PEACE IDEAS

Content Copyright © Paul Armstrong, August 2015. All Rights Reserved

TABLE OF CONTENTS

AFRICA

NIGERIA

Issues :

- Religious Terrorism

People Involved :

- Boko Haram
- Catholic Bishops Conference Of Nigeria
- Nasrul-Lahi Faith Society
- Nigerian Government
- Northern Nigerian States

Those Working For Peace :

- Interfaith Mediation Centre
- Nigerian Government
- The Foundation For Ethnic Harmony In Nigeria
- West African Network For Peacebuilding

SOMALIA

Issues :

- Civil War
- Divided Country : Autonomous Regions / Clan Areas / Areas Controlled By Rebels
- Imposition Of Islamic Laws
- Religious Extremism
- Weak Government

People Involved :

- African Union Mission In Somalia
- Al-Shabaab
- Eritrea Government
- Ethiopia Government
- Hizbul Islam
- Puntland State Of Somalia

- Somaliland Government

Those Working For Peace :

- Academy For Peace And Development Somaliland
- Forum For Peace And Governance (Somalia)
- Haqsoor
- Horn Peace
- Observatory Of Violence And Conflict Prevention
- Somalia Peace Network

SUDAN

Issues :

- Civil War
- Conflict Over Resources
- Displacement Of Peoples
- Imposition Of Islamic Laws
- Muslim - Christian Divide

People Involved :

- Darfur Region Peoples
- Government Of Republic Of Southern Sudan
- Rebel Movements
- Sudan Government

Those Working For Peace :

- Al Sarakmah Society
- Collaborative For Peace In Sudan
- Freedom Peace Equality Society
- Save Darfur
- South Sudan Centre For Conflict Resolution
- Sudan Interreligious Council
- Turath Organisation For Human Development
- Unity Community Organisation And Enlightment Trust

NIGERIA

Purpose : To negotiate a ceasefire with Boko Haram.

Strategy : In three parts - the first part provides what is on offer to Boko Haram. Part two provides suggestions on how to negotiate with Boko Haram. Part three provides sample letters to send address Boko Haram directly calling on them to commit to peace

<u>KEYWORDS</u>

"Boko Haram" "Disarmament" "Religion" "Muslim - Christian Holidays" "Terrorism List" "Prisoners" "Ceasefires" "Muslim Clerics" "Media" "Experts" "Mohammed" "Ethnic Cleansing"

"Political Wing"

13/05/2013 PAUL ARMSTRONG TO CHARGE D'AFFAIRES JOHN HENNESSEY-NILAND - PEACE IN NIGERIA

13/05/2013

TO US CHARGE D'AFFAIRES JOHN HENNESSEY

Dear Mr Hennessey-Niland,

I enclose some to ideas on negotiating with Boko Haram in Nigeria. They are good ideas. I had previously sent them to the Nigerian embassy in the UK to pass on to President Goodluck Jonathan. But I suspect he choose not to use them [for a reason ...] So I am asking you to pass these ideas on to your government and have your government work direct with the Nigerian government on bringing an end to the violence in Nigeria [using these ideas] If you like you can acknowledge this email.

God Bless

- Re: Disarmament -> Members hand their weapons over to their leaders and they hand them over to disarmament body OR a body of respected Muslims be set up to oversee that weapons are put "beyond use" by Boko Haram [in confidence]
- Religious groups can nominate people for election to local mayor
- Religious groups such as Boko Haram [if they become a religious group] can submit laws for parliament
- Tell Boko Haram : "Your actions have a "future" affect" | Tell them "Your violence will escalate into more than you intend

- Boko Haram will be allowed to travel to other countries during negotiations
- Get former terrorists elsewhere who have given up violence to talk to Boko Haram through the Nigerian government - The AIS - "Islamic Salvation Army" in Algeria; MB - "Muslim Brotherhood" / Egyptian Jihad / "Jama'ah Islamiya" in Egypt.
- Financial compensation for those who have been tortured or detained without charge
- Legalise their movement if turns to political methods [must have no more links to violence though]
- Encourage them to get involved in a cause other than religion -> prisoners rights / poverty / education / women's rights / corruption [This will draw them away from violence]
- Offer to publish Boko Haram's ideas / beliefs in the local media
- Financial support for pilgrimages to Mecca

- Make some / all Muslim Holidays national holidays in Nigeria - You may have to do the same for the Christian churches
- Admit mistakes made by Nigeria against Muslims to Boko Haram
- Doing good to people in their society / communities -> makes terrorists respect you : building mosques / providing Islamic textbooks
- Media access for Boko Haram / Islamist media funded by the government [Laws though : No incitement to hatred]
- Tell Boko Haram-> A reason to educate women is so they can teach their children
- Can meet religious leaders from other countries
- Boko Haram can produce its own media outlet [provided they promote peace in this outlet - their religious message can be free] - Point out to them they will get more followers if they do [the conditions is PROMOTION OF PEACE!]
- Offer Boko Haram a ceremony for the peace agreement between them and the government [Boko Haram gets publicity]

- If Boko Haram forms a political wing this wing would be allowed to fundraise in other countries
- Boko Haram can set up offices in other countries
- Setting up an Islamic Bank in the Northern Provinces
- Nigerian government getting other countries to remove Boko Haram from its "terrorism list"

- Sometimes the best way to diffuse a situation is not to react at all when someone says something negative

- Talk to Boko Haram prisoners in prison to get them to stick to a ceasefire - Stress to them 1. There is a purpose to a ceasefire 2. Peace talks will make real progress. 3. They do have capable negotiators on their side
- Socialise terrorists -> meeting lots of people [this will bring them out of isolation and make them more willing to turn to peace] -> government ministers / international figures / politicians / religious figures / human rights activists
- Tell them you will work with them where you can cooperate on issues -> get them involved with the government -> education : teaching Islam in classes / charitable works / social clubs for youths
- Get leaders of Boko Haram who choose peace to emphasise to their followers that they too have suffered and that they are committed Muslims
- Governments stressing you do not see disarmament as "surrender"
- Give more media access to moderate Muslim clerics in the country

- Terrorists want you to talk to them [Recognition]
- Negotiators : When you meet each side - provide other side with summary of discussion along with your own "helpful" commentary of discussion
- Talk about their families - to attackers - they can't live with this violence
- Say to them "You can unite people by showing your interest in them, by caring for them, by loving them. But you can't unite them by using violence on them. In fact instead of bringing people together; violence is widening the gap between them"
- Face issues truthfully but with respect
- Someone to take each side during negotiations - advise them and give them feedback [but they do not take part in the negotiations themselves
- Get an expert who has dealt with these kinds of issues before to talk to the two parties in the negotiations - provide their experiences

#8 20/04/2013 PAUL ARMSTRONG - TO PRESIDENT GOODLUCK EBELE JONATHAN - PEACE LETTER TO BOKO HARAM

20/04/2013
TO NIGERIAN PRESIDENT GOODLUCK EBELE JONATHAN

Dear Ambassador Tafida,
Please can you pass the following on to President Goodluck Ebele Jonathan.
I enclose a letter which I am asking you to pass on to Boko Haram. I also include all my previous

correspondence to you. I hope they prove helpful. This is my last email to you. If my ideas have proved helpful please write back to me.

Dear Sirs,

Listen - Pursue Islam peacefully. How can you share the message of Islam with others if you hate them and kill them. In the Koran Allah calls on people to know each other - this can only be achieved peacefully : "O you men! Surely we have created you of a male and a female, and made you into tribes and families that you may know each other." You can't unite people by force only Allah can unite people : "He it is who strengthened you with his help and with the believers. And united their hearts; Had you spent all that is in the earth, you could not have united their hearts, but Allah united them; Surely he is mighty, wise". You can have freedom to practice your religion and you can be safe. You can campaign for human rights and for more freedom to practice your religion. Choose peace - Islam really has only succeeded in spreading in the world where it was preached peacefully. There can be no turning back to violence if you choose peace you must give up arms - an international body of respected Muslims can supervise this.

#7 10/04/2013 PAUL ARMSTRONG - TO PRESIDENT GOODLUCK EBELE JONATHAN - PEACE LETTER TO BOKO HARAM

10/04/2013
TO NIGERIAN PRESIDENT GOODLUCK EBELE JONATHAN

Dear Ambassador Tafida,
Please can you pass the following on to President Goodluck Ebele Jonathan.
I enclose a letter which I am asking you to pass on to Boko Haram. I also include all my previous correspondence to you. I hope they prove helpful. I will be sending you another one email on bringing peace to Nigeria.
Dear Sirs,
Terrorism is not glamorous - it is violent and brutal. What if you were to choose peace? I have to say this : In the past some former fighters have gone on to be great peacemakers when they chose the path of peace. My hope is for you that you would choose the path of peace and persuade other fighters to end their campaigns. Now this is something Allah would approve of. The pursuit of peace is a noble cause. And yeah there are many injustices being perpetrated against Muslims around the world and I would like to see peace brought to these Muslim countries as well. I would like to point out : your organisation does not have to cease existing once there is peace -

it just has to have a new agenda; peace; the promotion of Islam [including charitable activities] and if you would like politics. You could do so much good - you have the religion which teaches you to do good works - but you have to give up arms there can be no turning back.

#6 31/03/2013 PAUL ARMSTRONG - TO PRESIDENT GOODLUCK EBELE JONATHAN - PEACE LETTER TO BOKO HARAM

31/03/2013
TO NIGERIAN PRESIDENT GOODLUCK EBELE JONATHAN

Dear Ambassador Tafida,
Please can you pass the following on to President Goodluck Ebele Jonathan. I enclose a letter which I am asking you to pass on to Boko Haram. I also include all my previous correspondence to you. I hope they prove helpful. I will be sending you another two emails on bringing peace to Nigeria.
Boko Haram - I will tell you what you are doing is hate not religion - the two are not compatible - Islam is a good religion and it is meant to be about peace and tolerance - Mohammed spoke of these two virtues repeatedly. I have seen Muslim extremists all over the world use the Koran to justify killing - strangely enough the Koran can also be used to speak about tolerance and peace - living with people of other religions including Christians. What does this mean - it means something is wrong - Allah does not contradict himself - he has not said one thing and then another - someone is wrong! Mohammed refers to Christians and Jews as people of the book. If you kill someone it is killing; if you kill someone it is killing - Allah will hold you to account. Now at the same time you must have some grievances; you want to protect your own religion - I have no problems with that! But the laws you apply to Muslims must not be applied to Non-Muslims in your areas - ethnic cleansing is a grave sin; it is one of the most serious sins you can commit. You have to live together - Christians and Muslims and Jews - racially / religiously pure - ethnic cleansing so there is only Muslims in your area and all Christians and Jews either killed of forced to leave is Hitler all over again! It is not too late to commit to real peace - And I would forgive you - I would even call on the government to allow an amnesty - maybe there can be some laws supporting the Muslim way of life in the

northern states where you are in a majority but these laws must not be enforced against non-Muslims - there must be tolerance - You have to live together and that is a permanent!

#5 21/03/2013 PAUL ARMSTRONG - TO PRESIDENT GOODLUCK EBELE JONATHAN - PEACE WITH BOKO HARAM

21/03/2013
TO NIGERIAN PRESIDENT GOODLUCK EBELE JONATHAN

Dear Ambassador Tafida,
Please can you pass the following on to President Goodluck Ebele Jonathan. I enclose ideas for negotiating with Boko Haram as well as all my previous correspondence to you. I hope they prove helpful. I will be sending you another three emails on bringing peace to Nigeria.

- Terrorists want you to talk to them [Recognition]
- Negotiators : When you meet each side - provide other side with summary of discussion along with your own "helpful" commentary of discussion
- Talk about their families - to attackers - they can't live with this violence
- Say to them "You can unite people by showing your interest in them, by caring for them, by loving them. But you can't unite them by using violence on them. In fact instead of bringing people together; violence is widening the gap between them"
- Face issues truthfully but with respect
- Someone to take each side during negotiations - advise them and give them feedback [but they do not take part in the negotiations themselves
- Get an expert who has dealt with these kinds of issues before to talk to the two parties in the negotiations - provide their experiences

#4 11/03/2013 PAUL ARMSTRONG - TO PRESIDENT GOODLUCK EBELE JONATHAN - PEACE WITH BOKO HARAM

11/03/2013
TO NIGERIAN PRESIDENT GOODLUCK EBELE JONATHAN

Dear Ambassador Tafida,
Please can you pass the following on to President Goodluck Ebele Jonathan. I enclose ideas for

negotiating with Boko Haram as well as all my previous correspondence to you. I hope they prove helpful. I will be sending you another four emails on bringing peace to Nigeria.

- Sometimes the best way to diffuse a situation is not to react at all when someone says something negative

- Talk to Boko Haram prisoners in prison to get them to stick to a ceasefire - Stress to them 1. There is a purpose to a ceasefire 2. Peace talks will make real progress. 3. They do have capable negotiators on their side

- Socialise terrorists -> meeting lots of people [this will bring them out of isolation and make them more willing to turn to peace] -> government ministers / international figures / politicians / religious figures / human rights activists

- Tell them you will work with them where you can cooperate on issues -> get them involved with the government -> education : teaching Islam in classes / charitable works / social clubs for youths

- Get leaders of Boko Haram who choose peace to emphasise to their followers that they too have suffered and that they are committed Muslims

- Governments stressing you do not see disarmament as "surrender"

- Give more media access to moderate Muslim clerics in the country

#3 1/03/2013 PAUL ARMSTRONG - TO PRESIDENT GOODLUCK EBELE JONATHAN - PEACE WITH BOKO HARAM

1/03/2013
TO NIGERIAN PRESIDENT GOODLUCK EBELE JONATHAN

Dear Ambassador Tafida,
Please can you pass the following on to President Goodluck Ebele Jonathan. I enclose ideas for negotiating with Boko Haram as well as all my previous correspondence to you. I hope they prove helpful. I will be sending you another five emails on bringing peace to Nigeria.

- If Boko Haram forms a political wing this wing would be allowed to fundraise in other countries
- Boko Haram can set up offices in other countries
- Setting up an Islamic Bank in the Northern Provinces

- Nigerian government getting other countries to remove Boko Haram from its "terrorism list"

19/02/2013

TO NIGERIAN PRESIDENT GOODLUCK EBELE JONATHAN

Dear Ambassador Tafida,

Please can you pass the following on to President Goodluck Ebele Jonathan. I enclose ideas for negotiating with Boko Haram as well as all my previous correspondence to you. I hope they prove helpful. I will be sending you another six emails on bringing peace to Nigeria.

- Make some / all Muslim Holidays national holidays in Nigeria - You may have to do the same for the Christian churches
- Admit mistakes made by Nigeria against Muslims to Boko Haram
- Doing good to people in their society / communities -> makes terrorists respect you : building mosques / providing Islamic textbooks
- Media access for Boko Haram / Islamist media funded by the government [Laws though : No incitement to hatred]
- Tell Boko Haram-> A reason to educate women is so they can teach their children
- Can meet religious leaders from other countries
- Boko Haram can produce its own media outlet [provided they promote peace in this outlet - their religious message can be free] - Point out to them they will get more followers if they do [the conditions is PROMOTION OF PEACE!]
- Offer Boko Haram a ceremony for the peace agreement between them

#1 13/02/2013 PAUL ARMSTRONG - TO PRESIDENT GOODLUCK EBELE JONATHAN - PEACE WITH BOKO HARAM

9/02/2013

TO NIGERIAN PRESIDENT GOODLUCK EBELE JONATHAN

Dear Ambassador Tafida,

Please can you pass the following on to President Goodluck Ebele Jonathan. I enclose ideas for negotiating with Boko Haram. I hope they prove helpful. I will be sending you another seven emails on bringing peace to Nigeria.

- Re: Disarmament -> Members hand their weapons over to their leaders and they hand them over to disarmament body OR a body of respected Muslims be set up to oversee that weapons are put "beyond use" by Boko Haram [in confidence]
- Religious groups can nominate people for election to local mayor
- Religious groups such as Boko Haram [if they become a religious group] can submit laws for parliament
- Tell Boko Haram : "Your actions have a "future" affect" | Tell them "Your violence will escalate into more than you intend"
- Boko Haram will be allowed to travel to other countries during negotiations
- Get former terrorists elsewhere who have given up violence to talk to Boko Haram through the Nigerian government - The AIS - "Islamic Salvation Army" in Algeria; MB - "Muslim Brotherhood" / Egyptian Jihad / "Jama'ah Islamiya" in Egypt.
- Financial compensation for those who have been tortured or detained without charge
- Legalise their movement if turns to political methods [must have no more links to violence though]
- Encourage them to get involved in a cause other than religion -> prisoners rights / poverty / education / women's rights / corruption [This will draw them away from violence]
- Offer to publish Boko Haram's ideas / beliefs in the local media
- Financial support for pilgrimages to Mecca

SOMALIA

Purpose : To negotiate a peace deal with Al-Shabaab and end all violence in Somalia. To heal the wounds of the people.

Strategy : To make Al-Shabaab feel that they can gain from negotiations. To reach out to them. To deal with the militias by talking to them and co-opting them. To make improvements in the Islamic nature of the state. To heal the divisions by creating Truth And Reconciliation Commissions; Involving Muslim clerics in human rights issues; visiting the people and listening to their stories.

KEYWORDS

"Saleh Mohammed" "TFG" "Al-Shabaab" "Eritrean Government" "Negotiations" "Islam" "Eritrean President Isaias Afewerki" "Sharia Laws" "Hisbul Islam" "Rotating Presidency" "Civil Society" "Clan Elders" "Puntland" "Jubba Valley region" "Mogadishu" "Symbolic Gestures" "Peace Conferences" "Somaliland" "OIC Countries"

1/12/2013 SOMALIA PEACE PROPOSAL IDEAS

01/12/2013

TALKING TO AL-SHABAAB

- Talking To Al-Shabaab
- Talk to al-shabaab about the past and the present :- what is wrong in society : militias/qat eating/constant outbreaks of violence between clans :- say we want to work together to fix this
- Ask al-shabaab who they want to work with them in negotiations :- organisation/country/individual clerics
- Ask them what other things besides sharia law are you interested in?
- Cite past examples to al-shabaab in which attacking groups in Somalia achieved concessions through negotiations
- Prioritize the demobilization of youth / people over a certain age / abducted people during negotiations in return for release of al-shabaab prisoners and the provision of food and medicine to al-shabaab as a confidence building measure. Also al-shabaab agrees to provide information it has on criminal gangs if it says it does not have links to criminal gangs.

- Agree to hold a referendum on highly contentious issues demanded by al-shabaab
- After a referendum al-shabaab agrees to demobilize all troops
- Somali government agrees to deal with corruption in justice / police and governance systems – work with international community and NGO's on this
- Somali government agrees to ask UN to remove al-shabaab leaders from UN sanctions list
- Al-shabaab can work on educational curriculum for children with government
- Tell al-shabaab a reason to educate women is so they can teach their children
- Al-shabaab appointed members to government can have a say in civil service, police and justice appointments
- Tell al-shabaab your goal of a "greater Somalia" would cost too much bloodshed.
- Somali government agrees to progressively change composition of AMISOM forces to forces from Muslim countries [Turkey / Pakistan / Libya]
- Each region decides on the level of sharia laws it wishes to implement
- Meet al-shabaab members in prison for negotiations
- Other groups part of negotiations along with government with Al-shabaab : - civil society / religious groups / elder members etc.

REACHING OUT TO AL-SHABAAB

- Somali government :- change the names and terms used to describe al-shabaab to more conciliatory terms [so they will choose peace] – don't use the word terrorist
- Acknowledge : when al-shabaab was part of Islamic Courts Union and controlled parts of Somalia that you were misrepresented by the western media – you were not as extreme as they made you out to be. Acknowledge : you did more than restore order when you were in

control. Actions such as returning properties taken by warlords to their rightful owners. You brought peace to the areas you controlled and Somalis WANT PEACE!

AMISOM FORCES

- AMISOM Forces :
- AMISOM troops moving their bases outside of cities into desert areas
- AMISOM forces in Somalia staying inside barracks : - only come out if there is renewed fighting between al-shabaab and government or if parts of the country become very unstable
- AMISOM forces may train local Somali forces
- AMISOM agrees not to attack where there are large civilian centres [Al-Shabaab agrees not to attack from large civilian centres] AMISOM will employ local militias in these areas. AMISOM agrees not to carry out aerial bombardments on large civilian centres

PEACE CONFERENCES

- Local peace conferences of elders appointing elders to a grand conference. NGO's providing logistics. Outsiders do not get involved in this process other than by providing financing
- For each peace conference :
- A preparatory committee :- formed to prepare an agenda, identify venues and secure funding for conferences
- Conference to be chaired by a non-voting committee
- Regional Conferences focus on regional issues first :- system of national politics/governance is not debated at regional conferences
- Independent observers present at conferences – including business people, poets, religious leaders, women
- Keep politicians out of the conferences – they only become involved in the implementation phase

PEACE AND HUMAN RIGHTS COMMISSIONS

- A peace commission comprised of Muslim clerics

- :- talking to militias to get them to give up violence – use religion as their argument
- :- providing safe passes/amnesties for al-shabaab members wishing to demobilise
- :- Being with the people – spending extended periods of time listening to people who have experienced loss, acknowledging the atrocities of war and conveying some sense of public outrage over the human loss
- :- pray with the locals + read the Koran before leaving such a situation
- :- peace commissions getting to meet government ministers
- A human rights commission within the Muslim church leadership

MILITIAS

- Stand up to the warlords – keep pursuing peace – they will be forced to come to the table eventually
- Somali militias allowed to keep some of their business interests
- Twice a week militia members can leave their work and go for education training
- Local residents getting to meet/talk to local faction leaders at a forum
- A public rally in various towns at which major streets are formally opened to the public [removal of checkpoints] Get women's groups involved in this
- Reduce the number of checkpoints to a few controllable legal barriers :- employ militias to man these checkpoints :- local administrations collect revenue from them
- If a militia breaks a ceasefire :
- They must hand over weapons used in violence to renew peace
- Other community members and members of their clan must also offer compensation to victims to secure peace deal
- Conflict resolution training for armed militias
- Bring business representatives and militia leaders together in workshops to discuss peace
- Each clan is responsible in its areas for :

- Dealing with the actions of bandits in their territories, each would establish a security council to oversee law and order, a clan-based police force would be created which would ultimately become part of a national police force
- Each community would disband their militias, arms would no longer be carried in urban areas or public gatherings

GOVERNANCE

- Government assisting in pilgrimages to Mecca
- Bring government and opposition together for public debates
- International donors pressuring Somali government to set up an anti-corruption commission + public expenditure reforms that track spending in all government departments : government works with donors on this
- Regional administrations hosting meeting of civil society actors to discuss peace, security and governance :- discuss how to achieve peace and reconciliation in region :- set up implementation committees :- broadcast the meetings on local radio stations to generate widespread public support for decisions made

PEACE

- Bring situation in Somalia to the international community – NGO's / Politicians
- A peace process in Somalia is going to take a few years
- Get former terrorists from other countries who have given up violence to talk to al-shabaab
- Get people to talk about what they experienced under al-shabaab to the media [government commits to protecting them]
- Businesses partnering and funding local NGOs
- Releasing high-level members of al-shabaab who are in prison for talks
- Truth And Reconciliation Commission [TRC]
    - Three committees : Amnesty committee; Reparation and Rehabilitation committee; and Human Rights violations committee.
    - Victims have their say at the TRC.
    - Offenders may have to make compensation to victims / return stolen property.
    - If offenders say all the crimes they committed and apologise to victims present at TRC they will be given amnesty.

- Muslim clerics can be involved in running the TRC
- Al-shabaab can set up an office in another Muslim country such as Qatar for negotiations with Somali government :- the office is not to be used for fundraising or propaganda
- Lots of witnesses to a peace agreement between Al-shabaab and Somalia government

SUDAN

Purpose : To achieve peace between Southern Sudan AND also to achieve peace between the government of Sudan and rebels in the provinces of Kordofan and Blue Nile.

Strategy : Re Peace between Sudan and Southern Sudan the strategy is get someone important involved and also use standard methods of negotiations [a UN mission to divide up the boundary areas] Re. Kordofan and the Blue Nile the strategy is to ease sanctions on Sudan in return for progress and to empower the rebels so much so that they are willing to negotiate

KEYWORDS

"President Omar Al-Bashir" "Kordofan" "Blue Nile" "Autonomy" "Religious Laws" "president Salva Kiir" "Southern Sudan" "Abyei"

3/9/2012 PAUL ARMSTRONG - TO AN TAOISEACH - PEACE IN SUDAN

3/09/2012

TO IRISH TAOISEACH ENDA KENNY

An Taoiseach,

I passed the following email on to the UK Sudanese embassy asking them to give it to the Sudan President Omar Al-Bashir. I hope it helps – please can you forward these ideas to the African Union – or whoever else you think should read this email.

3/9/2012 PAUL ARMSTRONG - TO SUDAN PRESIDENT OMAR AL-BASHIR

Dear Mr President,

I want peace. Alot of people are suffering in Kordofan and the Blue Nile because of the fighting. This war is not going to end any time soon. The international community is looking negatively at your country because of the fighting. There can be peace – if there is – there is alot to be gained from it. I have a number of suggestions. An intermediary acts as a go-between to negotiate with both sides; A venue outside the country hosts the talks. The international community in return for peace promises more aid both for the Sudan government and also for the regions in conflict. There would be disarmament of rebels. Many sanctions would be lifted by the international community. The rebel movements would be allowed to travel outside the country and meet others and talk to them while there is a ceasefire – this is a key idea here something that will go a long way to persuading them to commit to peace. The regions would be granted Autonomy – look to other examples of autonomy in the world to gain ideas for this. The regions would be

allowed to exercise their own religious laws. I will pass these ideas on to others as well.
Allah Bless You!

3/9/2012 PAUL ARMSTRONG - TO SUDAN PRESIDENT OMAR AL-BASHIR

3/09/2012

TO SUDAN GOVERNMENT PRESIDENT - OMAR AL-BASHIR

Dear Sir,

Please can you pass the following on to Sudan President Omar Al-Bashir.

Dear Mr President,

I want peace. Alot of people are suffering in Kordofan and the Blue Nile because of the fighting. This war is not going to end any time soon. The international community is looking negatively at your country because of the fighting. There can be peace – if there is – there is alot to be gained from it. I have a number of suggestions. An intermediary acts as a go-between to negotiate with both sides; A venue outside the country hosts the talks. The international community in return for peace promises more aid both for the Sudan government and also for the regions in conflict. There would be disarmament of rebels. Many sanctions would be lifted by the international community. The rebel movements would be allowed to travel outside the country and meet others and talk to them while there is a ceasefire – this is a key idea here something that will go a long way to persuading them to commit to peace. The regions would be granted Autonomy – look to other examples of autonomy in the world to gain ideas for this. The regions would be allowed to exercise their own religious laws. I will pass these ideas on to others as well.

Allah Bless You!

TO AN TAOISEACH - RE: PREVENTING WAR - SUDAN [SOMEONE IMPORTANT]

23/05/2011

TO IRISH GOVERNMENT

An Taoiseach,

I want to prevent a war in Sudan [north and south]. I propose that someone

IMPORTANT [a political leader] visits the two leaders such as UN secretary-general Ban Ki-moon. You are giving them attention [this psychological] it may just work – obviously the suggestions I sent to you in the two previous emails have to be implemented as well but maybe they need to hear it from someone IMPORTANT to move on the issue.

Sincerely

Save The World

AN TAOISEACH - RE: PREVENTING WAR BETWEEN SUDAN [NORTH AND SOUTH] - YOU CAN GET INVOLVED

23/05/2011

TO IRISH GOVERNMENT

An Taoiseach,

[Please let the Taoiseach read this letter today]

This is your chance to get involved – I sent the following email to the Sudanese president [northern Sudan] today. There is a danger of a war between the two parts of Sudan and I need your help to prevent it. I do not have a contact address for the southern Sudanese president – Can YOU contact him [president Salva Kiir] and pass on the message which I sent to the northern president on to him too. Would it [even getting the two sides talking to each other] what do you think? Talk to Egypt if you think this would be a good idea. Anything you can add to these ideas is welcome.

TO PRESIDENT OMAR AL-BASHAR

23/05/2011

TO SUDANESE GOVERNMENT

Dear Sir / Madam,

Can you pass the following on to President Omar Al-Bashir.

Dear Mr President

I want to help you. Re : southern Sudan – I don't think either of you [north or south] want war – You are talking BIG but neither of you wants war – You just need an opportunity for peace. I have a few suggestions – 1. both sides [military] should withdraw from Abyei – if possible the UN should stay in the town. 2. The UN should set up a body to decide how to demarcate ALL the total boundaries between your

two countries. 3. There should be positive gestures for peace – exchanging medicine / food – civilian groups can do this. 4. Talk to him your counterpart in the southern government. – You start by saying "I want peace"; "We are not going to change any previous agreements between our two peoples – Southern Sudan is still going to be independent"; [LIST THE THREE SUGGESTIONS I gave to you]; "We are linked together historically, economically, traditionally we should be friends". I Would Say These Things

ASIA

Afghanistan

Issues :

- Divided country - controlled by clans / warlords
- International NATO peacekeepers
- Religious terrorism
- War-Torn Country

People Involved :

- Afghan Government - Office Of The President
- NATO - Afghanistan International Security Assistance Force
- Taliban -[Wikipedia]

Those Working For Peace :

- Afghanistan Civil Society Forum Organization (ACSFO)
- Centre for Conflict and Peace Studies (CAPS)
- Cooperation for Peace and Unity (CPAU)

INDIA

Issues :

- Communist rebel insurgency
- Poverty
- Peasant rights

People Involved :

- Indian Government
- Communist Party Of India [Marxist]
- List of Naxalite and Maoist Groups in India

Those Working For Peace :

- Communist Party of India [Marxist]

Myanmar

Issues :

- Annulled Democratic Elections
- Imprisoned Democratic leader
- Military Dictatorship

People Involved :

- ASEAN
- Aung San Suu Kyi
- International Community
- Myanmar Government -[Ministry Of Foreign Affairs]

Those Working For Peace :

- Aung San Suu Kyi
- Burma Partnership
- Myanmar Peace Support Initiative

North Korea

Issues :

- Nuclear Weapons Testing - North Korea
- Communist Dictatorship - North Korea
- Impoverished Country - North Korea
- Unresolved Conflict between North and South Korea

People Involved :

- China Government
- North Korean Government
- South Korean Government
- USA

Those Working For Peace :

- Korean Peninsula Energy Development Organisation
- International Liaison Committee for Reunification and Peace in Korea

PAKISTAN / INDIA

Issues :

- Contested Territory - Kashmir
- Terrorism
- Nuclear Arms Race

People Involved :

- India Government
- Kashmir Terrorists
- Pakistan Government

Those Working For Peace :

- India-Pakistan Peace
- Pakistan-India Peoples Forum For Peace And Democracy

Pakistan Internal

Issues :

- Corruption
- Religious Extremism
- Persecution of Christian minorities
- Religious Terrorism
- Women's Rights

People Involved :

- Pakistan Christian Churches -[Pakistan Christian Concern]
- Pakistan Government
- Pakistan Judiciary -[Supreme Court Of Pakistan]
- Pakistan Political Parties -[Wikipedia]
- Pakistani Terrorists

Those Working For Peace :

- Pakistan Institute For Peace Studies
- Peace Network Pakistan
- **National Commission For Peace And Justice**
- The Centre For Peace And Development Initiatives -[CPDI-Pakistan]

Sri Lanka

Issues :

- Discrimination against minorities
- A War weary people [Tamils]
- An over zealous buddhist community

People Involved :

- Sri Lanka Government
- Tamil political parties
- Indian government

Those Working For Peace :

- Indian government
- Sri Lanka Campaign For Peace & Justice
- Association Of War Affected Women
- Campaign For Free And Fair Elections
- Center For Peace And Reconciliation
- Centre For Human Rights And Research
- Janakaraliya
- Jeeva Jothy
- Jeewa Shakthi Foundation
- Kaveri Kala Manram
- National Ethnic Unity Foundation
- National Peace Council
- Samadeepa
- Samasevaya
- Shanti Community Animation Movement

AFGHANISTAN

Purpose : To get the Taliban to end violence and negotiate with the Afghan government

Strategy : Provide ways of inserting Islamic values into the governance system while still respecting human rights and civil society

KEYWORDS

"Religious Practices / Ceremonies" "UN Radio Station" "NWFP" "Peace" "Reconciliation" "Culture" "Religion" "Extremism" "Red Cross" "Taliban leader Mullah Omar" "ISAF" "Taliban Prisoners" "Muslim Religious Councils" "Education System"

AFGHANISTAN PEACE PROPOSAL

1/01/2014

COMMITTING TO PEACE

- Taliban must cut its ties with Al-Qaeda
- Taliban must eject all non-Taliban terrorist leaders from Afghanistan
- Acknowledge positive traits of Taliban: - They want peace too – they just want the ISAF gone and sharia included in the constitution. They want good relations with other foreign countries. They want to deal with the issue of corruption in society and governance.
- Tell the Taliban – a reason to educate girls is so they can teach their children
- Tell Taliban leader Mullah Omar : You once said you had a dream – "I had a dream – I dreamed that the holy Prophet [Muhammed] appeared before me and said we must bring peace"

CONCESSIONS TO TALIBAN

- Financial settlement for families of Taliban members if they demobilise in a peace agreement
- A financial settlement for the Taliban as a whole
- Release of Taliban prisoners in other countries
- Removal of the Taliban and its leadership from the UN terrorist list

- Taliban can publish their ideas in the media
- Access for Taliban to some foreign governments if they commit to a ceasefire

PEACE STRUCTURE

- Turkey/Saudi Arabia/USA/Russia/China/Pakistan sending delegations to talks: - interacting with Taliban/Afghan negotiators on sides of talks: - placing incentives/putting pressure on sides to reach a deal
- OIC [Organisation of Islamic Conference] to host talks between Taliban and Afghan government
- OIC puts forward a peace plan
- International community recognising a peace agreement

PEACE IDEAS

- Imams allowed to govern local villages/towns/small cities with a Muslim religious council
- OIC to send a fact-finding delegation composed of foreign ministers from several OIC countries: - visit communities | talk to local Taliban commanders
- OIC with negotiating parties must decide and agree at start on areas to be negotiated on
- Islamic values that Taliban wish to see included in education system incorporated gradually after researches and studies are conducted
- Educational programs may vary from region to region
- Each region can vote and decide on its own level of sharia laws
- OIC to recognise the Taliban
- At some stage the president of Afghanistan gets involved in the peace talks
- Islamic clerics can enter politics
- Agree to work with international community / NGO's to end corruption in the police / judiciary / and politics
- Bring forward a presidential election / parliamentary elections to a few months after a peace agreement OR form an interim government with positions in government given to Taliban members
- Get people from other conflicts who have achieved peace to talk to the sides [Taliban / Afghan government]

- Provide people with choice about where to go to seek justice :- Taliban style courts [sharia courts] / elder councils / police officials / state courts
- Replace High Peace Council in negotiations with Taliban with a team of government ministers AND this government team may include religious leaders
- A referendum on the peace agreement
- A civil society assembly meeting before talks begin with Taliban that puts forward issues and recommendations to be discussed at peace conference
- To reduce numbers in the ANA [Afghan National Army] place more of its members into a reserve force instead

DEMOBILIZATION

- Taliban fighters amalgamated into army can join at same rank they held in their organisation
- Groups of communities holding a peace meeting together and agreeing to disarm Taliban in their area – Get financing from government to do this [plus incentives]. NGO's + local government also involved in disarmament with local communities and UN observers [non-military] also present

INDIA

Purpose : To end the naxalite rebellion by reaching out to them and addressing their goals

Strategy : Addressing the naxalite demands of land, dignity and wages for all peasants. Empowering women - important in preventing communism from spreading

KEYWORDS

"Digital Registry Of Land" "Corruption In Politics" "Media" "Police" "Naxalites" "Schools" "Dalit" "Land Rights" "Landlords" "Communism" "Democracy" "Peace Zones" "Credit Unions" "Social Welfare Payments" "Landless peasants" "Research Institute on poverty" "Parliament" "Congress Of Nations" "Prisoners"

#11 PEACE TALKS WITH THE NAXALITES - PAUL ARMSTRONG

19/07/2015

TO INDIAN GOVERNMENT

Dear Ambassador,

I enclose more ideas for brining peace with the Naxalites - This is my final email to you on this subject. I also enclose all my previous correspondence to you.

- Digital registry of all lands owned by peasants
- A 5% tax for the poor on the middle and upper classes similar to the Muslim system of Zakat [5% also]
- If as a peasant you have been on the land for a number of years the land becomes yours
- Agricultural colleges / local courses in the villages [a few weeks]
- Landlord organises feasts a few times a year to all his workers
- Landlords pay in cash to peasants
- Middlemen agree to pay a certain wage to peasants at start of planting season - the payment is guaranteed
- Auctioning of produce to middlemen by peasants to get the best prices
- Unused land must be sold to peasants
- Landlords can pay their tenants in land rather than money
- Companies leasing lands of peasants who stay on the land as employees - so companies can create plantations

- Someone in the village such as a teacher - reads the news in the newspapers to those who are illiterate
- A lead farm - introducing new techniques [trained by government - they then pass this knowledge onto other farmers
- The eldest son / daughter inherits the land - cannot keep breaking up the land into smaller proportions

#10 PEACE TALKS WITH THE NAXALITES - PAUL ARMSTRONG</h3>

30/05/2015

TO INDIAN GOVERNMENT

Dear Ambassador,

I enclose ideas for dealing with corruption in politics. Corruption is an issue that the Naxalites argue over. I also enclose all my previous correspondence to you. I have passed these ideas on to the communist party of India as well. Work together on this.

CORRUPTION IN POLITICS
- A branch within the police specifically to investigate corruption
- Business can fill out government forms over the internet to avoid levels of corruption
- Media publicizing corruption
- A judicial body to investigate corruption
- Rewards for reporting corruption if it shows to be true
- A business integrity forum - to ensure businesses do not have to give bribes to people.
- Employ foreigners alongside judiciary to investigate corruption
- Politicians can register to have their finances investigated by the judiciary - Establish their credentials as "clean" politicians
- Politicians including the president cannot have shares or ownership over state assets
- Establish a citizen report card - to survey citizens opinions / experiences of various state companies / state ministries. The results would be publicised in the media
- A UN workshop on corruption for politicians in the country
- A minister for corruption - drawn from civil society

- An international court in the country to deal with corruption; validating elections - Reasons for this local judiciary is not skilled enough - concerns that local judiciary may not be as efficient due to lack of funding
  - International police training for investigations / audits of people's finances
- Community groups - individuals joining together when seeking financing / applications for services - may reduce corruption
  - NGO's can talk direct to the president about corruption
  - Appointing judiciary with approval of parliament
- A tracking survey - how much of government funding budgeted for schools, health
- clinics etc. actually reaches them - citizens monitoring the budget
  - Party financing must be made public - who supported them
  - Political parties must have a party support base of people | must garner at least 5,000 signatures to form a party
  - Political leaders must have their finances investigated
  - Protect those in the civil service who expose corruption
- Media presence at court cases | especially corruption cases
  - Media can have access to public service to audit where money is being "lost" along the chain of bureaucracy
- Must vote for a party rather than individual politicians - reduces corruption such
- as buying votes / politicians doing favours for people
  - Making people aware of the consequences of corruption. They will be less likely to give in to corruption or accept it
- Force new legislation on corruption by gathering votes from across the political divide in parliament

#9 PEACE TALKS WITH THE NAXALITES - PAUL ARMSTRONG

28/05/2015

TO INDIAN GOVERNMENT

Dear Ambassador,

When negotiating with the Naxalites - the issue of police corruption can be brought up and you can list the suggestions below that you intend to use to tackle this issue.

POLICE CORRUPTION

- Rotating police officers between districts to reduce corruption
- Vary police officers roles
- Full screening of backgrounds of recruits to the police force
- Candidates with higher levels of education should be sought and those who continue their education should be rewarded
- A use of a polygraph testing in initial screenings of candidates
- Police commanders are held personally responsible for their subordinates actions with regard to corruption
- Community policing begins after extensive training where police officers spend several days conducting surveys at each residence and business in their assigned neighbourhood. There are two purposes for this 1. To introduce police officers to community residences and generate public interest 2. They provide officers with a preliminary assessment of the principal concerns specific to the community - providing info not just on citizen security but other social problems as well.
- An external commission to monitor police - independent of governance; must publicize findings
- Start from the top down. Police commanders must be seen visibly and persistently to lead reform. Reinforce the message by personal visits to the rank and file police stations
- Reformers must think of ways to remind officers about what is expected in particular situations
- Signs can be placed at receiving counters at police stations that complaints must be registered without monetary charge
- Police should develop programs informing the public about anti-corruption initiatives and publicize procedures for complaining - This may raise anxiety among police officers that people will complain
- Police showing sincere efforts at reform will gain more respect from the public - giving them a sense of pride. Policing then becomes a vocation rather than a job
- Bring together police officer and civil society representatives to overcome a legacy of suspicion and fear. Participants in these dialogues exchange information about the sources of crime and violence and

discussed ways that the police best re-establish control in the community. These dialogues should be renewed and continue

#8 PEACE TALKS WITH THE NAXALITES - PAUL ARMSTRONG

28/05/2015

TO INDIAN GOVERNMENT

Dear Ambassador,

I enclose more ideas for bringing peace with the Naxalites - I have also passed these ideas on to the communist party.

<u>JUSTICE</u>

- If politicians made trafficking and slavery a national issue the police would be forced to act
- Arrest the customers who use brothels not the girls / women
- Giving young children a shelter they can use as an address with their own individual postal box
- Reward those involved in social justice
- Turn former brothels into schools - Sex workers they one thing they say is "save our
- children"
- In seeking justice for women abused / raped - they should ask a local politician to go with them to the police

<u>FINANCING</u>

- Indigenous NGO's establishing offices in western countries for fundraising
- Get the president of India involved - he should have a presidential fund which he can use to help others such as women and children

<u>DIGNITY</u>

- Give young children school uniforms - A study in South Africa found that giving uniforms [especially to young girls] increased the likelihood of children staying in
- school. So they marry at a later age and there are reduced pregnancies
- A university for women
- Studies of women from China, Rwanda, Namibia show that educating and employing women can be a significant boost to the country's economy

#7 PEACE TALKS WITH THE NAXALITES - PAUL ARMSTRONG

27/05/2015

TO INDIAN GOVERNMENT

Dear Ambassador,

I enclose more ideas for bringing peace with the Naxalites - I have also passed these ideas on to the communist party.

DIGNITY

- Politicians attending dalit schools on graduation day
- Encourage Dalit children to aspire to a better life - bring people of different professions to talk to gatherings of Dalit children
- Organize sports competitions for dalit children - give them something of a childhood

WAGES

- Address this to Bollywood - make films and give the profits to charity

JUSTICE

- Indigenous NGO's going abroad to tell the stories of peasants and dalits to international media
- Boycott Hindu temples that refuse to accept Dalits
- Show people on TV the good work that is being done in your country for Dalits
- Recruit third level students into NGO's - it must be part of their course [Mandatory]

#6 PEACE TALKS WITH THE NAXALITES - PAUL ARMSTRONG

26/05/2015

TO INDIAN GOVERNMENT

Dear Ambassador,

I enclose more ideas for bringing peace with the Naxalite fighters. I am also passing these ideas on to the communist party. Work together to bring peace

DIGNITY

- Training midwifes for each village at least two of them
- Access points in cities for people to get clean water
- Free children's books for rural areas - to help children to learn
- The Catholic church / protestant churches working on social justice - they are good at this

POLITICS

- Get trade unionists to join politics
- Communities eat together on a certain day each week [People's kitchens] - sponsored by landlords - for organizing together to achieve their rights

- Invite bureaucrats to people's kitchens - less likely to be involved in corruption if they get to know the locals

LAND

- Land reform - peasants [who now own the land] promise to sell to former landlords who then sell it to the market
- Community ownership of land - share the profits

#5 PEACE TALKS WITH THE NAXALITES - # PAUL ARMSTRONG

13/05/2015

TO INDIAN GOVERNMENT

Dear Ambassador,

I enclose more ideas for bringing peace with the Naxalite fighters. I am also passing these ideas on to the communist party. Work together to bring peace.

WAGES

- Landlords must give one months salary to landless labourers when they are no longer needed
- Philanthropy Unions - of rich people and rich companies
- Companies must pay a certain amount of money to people on strike

DIGNITY

- A peace march from one side of the country to the other - calling for an end to the naxalite rebellions and calling for major land reform
- Investigate armed groups maintained by Landlords after an amnesty on the issue - charge those who still maintain them
- Break up states in some parts of the country into more states - bringing government closer to the people
- Registering poor people - giving birth certs. A computer database of land ownership in each state
- Collective protests where children have been taken into bonded labour to pay bills - supported by politicians
- Wives of politicians can register themselves as politicians [without election] in state and federal governments
- Women should hold deeds to land as well as husbands

LAND

- Zoning agricultural land - more food for people less cash crops
- Very long term low interest loans [30 - 40 years] from the government to peasants to buy their land

- Landlords incomes will be tax free if they sell their land [incentive for them to sell to peasants]

#4 PEACE TALKS WITH THE NAXALITES - PAUL ARMSTRONG

30/04/2015

TO INDIAN GOVERNMENT

Dear Ambassador,

This is my fourth email to you in negotiating with the Naxalites. Please pass these on to the Indian government. I am also passing these ideas on to the communist party. Work together for peace.

DIGNITY

- Say positive things about communism while supporting democracy
- Naxalites apologize for civilian casualties
- Politicians symbolically accepting books on communism from Naxalites
- Human rights NGO's can go into prisons and visit Naxalite prisoners
- Make national leaders visit Bihar and other places see how much the people are suffering - perhaps it may motivate them to do more for the poor. India can afford it.

LAND

- Each dalit on landlords land must have and OWN their own patch of land - just enough to feed his family
- Peace zones - no Senas; no soldiers or paramilitary soldiers and no Naxalites in these areas. Peace zones are chosen by the people themselves. This has been done in Colombia in the past with some success. Large groups of unarmed peasants organize to defend their peace zones by their simple presence in large numbers.

WAGES

- The best way out of poverty is credit unions. Unfortunately a common problem with third world countries is corruption. I propose that the government funds in banks directly transfer money to local credit unions for village councils to use thus eliminating corruption at the different levels. Since it would cost too much to provide regular social welfare - I propose that the government via such credit unions would make a larger payment 4 - 5 a year to families. Also with education - parents could be paid a small stipend every two month [a weeks wages] for sending their children to school [all the way to completing secondary school]. This also they would receive via the credit union. Also the children can receive free school lunches. Establishing credit union centres must be your number one priority.

- Pay villagers to hand in weapons - de-escalate the problem

<u>JUSTICE</u>

- Free legal aid centers across the land

#3 PEACE TALKS WITH THE NAXALITES - PAUL ARMSTRONG

28/04/2015

TO COMMUNIST PARTY OF INDIA [MARXIST]

Dear Mr. Bardhan,

I enclose a third email to you for negotiating with the Naxalites. Based on the concepts of Dignity / land / wages / Justice. I want you to know I am also passing these ideas on to the government - work together on peace.

<u>DIGNITY</u>

- Give untouchables and dalits more respectful names - A change of name will give them dignity
- Find quotes in the Sanskrit that support untouchables
- Encourage Brahmans to support the rights of untouchables
- Government in Bihar acknowledge the suffering and wrongs done to the poor
- A day of mourning for Dalits who have suffered from violence - Politicians attending these meetings and pledging to make reforms

<u>LAND</u>

- If landlords do not live on land they must sell it to the government
- Maybe government cannot provide lands but houses for landless can be built on landlords land where they work.

<u>WAGES</u>

- Promise to provide education for landless peasants - free school lunches | a small stipend [value of 1 weeks wages per month] to the family if they send their children to school
- Village leaders with more powers can raise a very small tax on local landlords
- Instead of regular social welfare payments which the government cannot afford provide larger grants four to five times a year

<u>JUSTICE</u>

- Congress / BJP choosing peasants [dalits] as candidates for elections
- Student's speaking out for peasant rights of the landless especially
- Police must come from the local area
- Compensation for those arrested but not convicted / charged
- Registering dalits electronically - with passport photo as ID

- ## A research institute on peasants issues

- ## Senior police officers from other states directing the local police to deal with corruption and suspected officers working with the Senas

#2 PEACE TALKS WITH THE NAXALITES - PAUL ARMSTRONG

25/04/2015

TO COMMUNIST PARTY OF INDIA [MARXIST]

Dear Sir / Madam,

Dear Mr. Bardhan,

I enclose my second email on peace with the Naxalites. Here I provide ideas for negotiating a ceasefire.

NEGOTIATING IDEAS

I enclose a list of ideas on a strategy for negotiating with terrorists. I hope it works!

- Acknowledge wrongs have been committed [to the insurgent group]
- [to insurgent group] Talk to the people you claim to represent – ask them for their opinions – should you negotiate
- Point out to them all terrorist movements move from violence to peace eventually
- Say to them there is a lot of work to be done – even after a ceasefire and peace
- Tell them - If you turn to peace – you can be a lobby movement for your cause – you will probably get more support – model yourself on other peaceful communist movements
- Point out to them – now is the best time in history to negotiate
- Ask them what progress they have achieved with violence – not a lot
- Tell them submit your ideas to the public at large
- Tell them you want more members – you are going to have to choose the path of peace
- Tell them you are going to have to talk to other groups – DIALOGUE

- Acknowledge the wrongs that have been committed [to the insurgent group]
  - I know that you have some just grievances; we have committed wrongs. People have been hurt. But now we want peace. Will you talk to us. The reason you started fighting was

because you perceived injustices and wanted to protest against them. Now I am telling you – you can end those injustices and achieve a just peace by talking to us.

- [to insurgent group] Talk to the people you claim to represent – ask them for their opinions – should you negotiate
  - Talk to those you represent ask them what they think of the situation. Ask the people on the ground from your community do you want us to negotiate – do you want us to continue fighting. Are you tired of the suffering. Do you trust us to come up with a just settlement for you
- Point out to them all terrorist movements move from violence to peace eventually
  - I wish to point out to you – History does repeat itself – all terrorist movements eventually move from fighting to pursuing peace. In the end you too will choose peace it is just a matter of when. Time and again terrorists have realised that there actions stand to succeed more if they turn from violence to peace. Yes violence gave them a voice – but it will not gain them an agreement for that they need to pursue peace.
- Say to them there is a lot of work to be done – even after a ceasefire and peace
  - Even when you do choose peace – there is still a lot of work to be done. We need to rebuild this country – heal the wounds of hatred and grief. We need to reintegrate former fighters into peaceful activities. You are a part of this future.
- Tell them - If you turn to peace – you can be a lobby movement for your cause – you will probably get more support – model yourself on other peaceful communist movements
  - If you turn to peace – you can enter politics – you will be able to talk to the media freely – you will be listened to by a greater audience. You will be heard. You will achieve progress. Please model yourself on other communist movements such as the Communist Party India [Marxist]. Who knows you may even end up in a coalition government some day.
- Point out to them – now is the best time in history to negotiate
  - Now is the best time to negotiate – People are tired of the violence on all sides. There are elements of people ready to listen and negotiate on all sides –politicians have become pragmatic – they know they have to talk to you – that the fighting is only leading to a stalemate. This was not so in the past.
- Ask them what progress they have achieved with violence – not a lot
  - What progress have you made using violence – Not a lot. You have been fighting for several years now. All I see is a war of attrition with neither side able to defeat the other completely. If you do not try and take the peace option what does the future hold for you - only continued strife and suffering for everyone.
- Tell them submit your ideas to the public at large
  - If you choose peace – you will be given the opportunity to submit your ideas to the public at large. You will be addressing more people than you ever have before and what's more

the press will not be reporting you in a hostile way instead in an open business like way. But you must choose peace for this to happen.

- Tell them - you want more members – you are going to have to choose the path of peace
  - You are not a large organisation – at least not directly speaking and the people are getting tired of violence – that's where the majority of people lie. If you wish to become a bigger organisation and have a real voice – if you wish to recruit more members you are going to have to choose the path of peace.
- Tell them - you are going to have to talk to other groups – DIALOGUE
  - You cannot act in isolation forever – you need to broaden your base; you want other people to listen to you – you are going to have to talk to other groups – This means dialogue – To come out of this isolation you must choose peace.

PEACE TALKS WITH THE NAXALITES - PAUL ARMSTRONG

17/04/2015

TO COMMUNIST PARTY OF INDIA [MARXIST]

Dear Sir / Madam,

I need your help in ending the Naxalite insurgency. I have some experience at working on peace in the world - you can check out my website if you wish http://www.peace-implementation.info/downloads.html

I will be sending you two more emails on this topic one on negotiating a ceasefire and the other on a letter addressed to the communist party [Maoist] + Naxalite insurgents.

IDEAS:

- **Naxalite leaders to address national parliament**

- **Naxalite leaders can appoint positions to judiciary / human rights boards, government ministries instead of you taking them yourselves**

- Allow your ideas to be published in the national media

- Broadcast the negotiations on television and local radio

- Get members in prison to call for talks with government - There is a purpose, you will get concessions.

- A congress of nations from the south-east asia region - Nepal, Sir lanka, India, Bangladesh, Pakistan on peace development and social justice

- **Government immediately sets up a peace congress before talks with Naxalite-Maoists**

- A regional vote for peace in areas affected by Naxalites

- A camp for Naxalite-Maoists where social leaders, representatives of political organisations, and ordinary people can come to make contact with insurgents and start debates with guerrillas
- Provide legal advice centres across the country
- Since there is no social welfare for the poor - the government should LARGER grants to people - 4 to 5 times a year.
- Assistance for rebel members released from prison.
- School feeding programmes for children who attend school - children more likely and be sent by parents
- A LARGE government fund to finance NGO projects
- Cancel all debts owed by peasants to government "an amnesty"
- A peasants institute for policy development, research, empowering peasants
- Civil society putting forward suggestions and issues for talks process
- Leaders of the insurgency can consult with civil society committee set up by civil society forum
- Insurgents can meet informally with other communist parties
- Local communities involved in recruiting members to police forces

MYANMAR

Purpose : To persuade the Myanmar government to allow in foreign aid agencies

Strategy : Tell the Myanmar government that other countries just as *"cautious"* as you have allowed in foreign aid agencies when they needed the help.

<u>KEYWORDS</u>

"Aung San Suu Kyi" "NLD" "Elections" "Amnesty For Political Prisoners" "General Than Shwe" "The Constitution" "Referendum" "Buddhists"

CONSTITUTION - FOREIGN AID

11/05/2008

TO MYANMAR GOV. [un mission]

Dear Ambassador,

I hope you pass this on to your leader Than Shwe.

Dear Mr. Shwe

Everyone asks for help when they need it. I know you have accepted help from your friends - but right now everyone wants to help you. I know you are concerned about spying - you have to realise that the many aid agencies have gone to many other countries all cautious like yours and accepted help. Find a way to let the agencies in - talk to the UN and come to an agreement where the UN and other aid workers can enter your country - temporarily of course.

NORTH KOREA

Purpose : To end nuclear testing in North Korea and to improve relations between North and South Korea

Strategy : Encouraging the North Korean leadership to leave the door open on the possibility of negotiations given the right circumstances. Encouraging the US to be more flexible in negotiations and providing them with some negotiating strategies. Laying the case to the North Koreans that no one should be proud of having nuclear weapons

KEYWORDS

"Military Negotiations" "Military Exercises" "Nuclear Free Zone" "IAEA"

"Anti-American Propaganda" "President Kim Jong-II"

22/04/2013 PAUL ARMSTRONG - TO US CHARGE D'AFFAIRES FOR IRELAND JOHN HENNESSEY - PEACE IN NORTH KOREA

22/04/2013

TO US PRESIDENT BARACK OBAMA

Dear Mr Hennessey,

Please can you pass the following on to President Barack Obama [directly not to anyone else]. I have provided a list of ideas on achieving peace with North Korea. One idea I would really like you to try out is to turn the two Koreas into an area where there are no armies at all. If you are passing on these ideas please confirm this to me either in writing or by email.

NEGOTIATIONS

- ## Mlitary[US] to Military Discussions / Negotiations [NK]

- US keeps South Korea informed of its talks with North Korea

- US holds direct talks with NK on military issues while SK negotiates with NK on all other issues

- NK may be changeable in its statements – you must be consistent keep up pursuing peace

PEACE IDEAS

- NK wants unification just as much as SK

- A single currency for North and South Korea [on one side same image on the other side national image : similar to the euro] | A single central bank to prevent either side from mass producing currency

- South Korea / US diplomatic [ambassadorial] relations with North Korea + North Korean relations with US

- No military exercises on either side any more

- South Korea to allow more communist parties to run in elections
- NK and SK to have no armies at all and all foreign armies to be removed [TRY THIS !!]
- Address NK by its formal name : "Democratic People's Republic Of Korea"
- IAEA inspectors for SK nuclear reactors as well

PRECEDENT :

- NK in negotiations : talks to a council from south consisting of political parties / social groups and government [This was an NK suggestion in 1992]
- An NK proposal from 1992 was for a three stage integration of NK and SK – Stage 1 can be implemented Now!
- Stage 1 – Formation of a confederation of republics in which both parties retain sovereignty
- Stage 2 – A federal system composed of one federation and two local governments
- Stage 3 – Complete unification leaving one nation, one state, one government
- A nuclear free-zone in Korea suggested in 1991 by vice-minister Chon In Chol in talks with Japanese foreign minister Nakahira Noboru

The key thing with all these precedents is to say that it was your side that suggested these ideas

US DEMANDS ON NK :

- Improve relations with SK tangibly
- Cooperate in full with the IAEA and on all nuclear treaties
- Account for US soldiers missing in action during the Korean war
- Other confidence building measures including restraint on the sale of arms abroad
- Cease its anti-American propaganda
- Ensure that NK does not support international terrorism

If NK implements any of these six points the US will take reciprocal positive steps

TO NORTH KOREAN GOVERNMENT

19/10/2006

TO NORTH KOREA GOV. [north Korea government]

What would make you change course and cease the development of nuclear weapons? You want the wellbeing and security of your people first. Leave open the possibility that you "could" disarm your nuclear weapons given the right circumstances - Lets start with that - Maybe you could indicate to the international community that you are flexible.

TO IRISH GOVERNMENT RE: NORTH KOREA ACTIONS

19/10/2006
TO IRISH GOV. [irish government]

What do you think - Are North Korea's actions a form of protest suicide at the plight of their people. Could the offer of investment and development help persuade the North Koreans to change course.

I sent the following to korea@korea-dpr.com [Government website]
What would make you change course and cease the development of nuclear weapons? You want the wellbeing and security of your people first. Leave open the possibility that you "could" disarm your nuclear weapons given the right circumstances - Lets start with that - Maybe you could indicate to the international community that you are flexible.

HOW TO IMPROVE RELATIONS WITH NORTH KOREA

19/10/2006
IRISH GOV. [irish government]

I think we should move back to a point where relations with North Korea were improving. Three aspects helped ease tensions with North Korea in the past

- 1. Food aid and economic aid in return for a suspension of its nuclear program.
- 2. Sending Jimmy Carter as an envoy of the US government – North Korea

Lifting of all trade sanctions and economic investment in return for disarmament of weapons and nuclear facilities. You can point out to the North Koreans that economic investment will strengthen their economy and enable them to stand on firmer ground. Somebody needs to talk to them and keep the lines of communication open even now with the sanctions and nuclear tests. The biggest challenge lies with MR. Bush in March 2001 "Bush holds a summit with South Korean president Kim Dae Jung in Washington. Although he publicly endorses the Sunshine Policy, privately Bush tells Kim that the U.S. will not continue talks with North Korea, setting aside the Clinton administration's policy of engagement. The South Korean president is stunned." North Korea wants to hold talks directly with the US.

PAKISTAN – INDIA

Purpose : To resolve the Kashmir Dispute and abolish nuclear weapons in the world

Strategy : Offering incentives. Using ideas already known. Providing solutions to autonomy questions.

<u>KEYWORDS</u>

<h3>"Richard Holbrooke" "Kashmir" "Tribal Regions" "Al-Qaeda" "The Taliban" "President Asif Ali Zardari" "Lashkar E. Taiba" "India" "Pakistan" "NWFP" "PMLN Party" "Prime Minister Nawaz Sharif" "Referendum" "President Pervez Musharraf" "Organisation Of Islamic Countries [OIC]" "Pakistan Christian Church"

PAUL ARMSTRONG - PEACE IN KASHMIR

18/04/2015

TO INDIA GOV. [Irish Embassy]

Your excellency Mrs. Radhika Lal Lokesh,

Please pass these ideas on to your government. I provide you with some ideas for peace in Kashmir and peace between Pakistan and your country.

- Kashmir can make its own laws and the indian constitution should be minimized in the region
- Kashmir can have its own flag provided that it is a variation on the Indian flag.
- Kashmir can have official titles such as prime minister
- Launch a campaign against corruption in the state
- No religious laws however both muslims and hindus would be able to celebrate their own religious holidays in their own majority areas of Jammu and Kashmir
- Kashmir can create its own taxes
- Members of Kashmir parliament may also at the same time be members of the indian or pakistani parliaments.
- Pakistan and India agree to reduce tariffs on each others goods
- Meet with all political parties in Pakistan - talk to them about these ideas. A platform of support for peace talks would help. This needs to be done for Pakistan.

PAUL ARMSTRONG - PEACE + NUCLEAR WEAPONS

31/03/2015

TO INDIA GOV. [Irish Embassy]

Your excellency Mrs. Radhika Lal Lokesh,

Please pass these ideas on to your government.A few proposals here on Kashmir – share this region with Pakistan – Free travel to the region from both Pakistan and India. It would have its own autonomous government [with certain powers]. I want you to note that before former

President Musharraf left office he was close to a deal with you along these lines. An investment board matched rupee for rupee by both Pakistan and India to encourage people to stay in the region. Check out my link <a href="http://www.peace-implementation.info/employment_ideas.html" Employment ideas for ideas on generating employment. Consider these ideas a reward for making peace. I update this site every so often so check back at least once every three months for more ideas. Also as a reward if you make peace here I will work on ending the Naxalite-Maoist insurgency in your country. PROMISE!

A body such as the non-aligned movement could appoint ministers or the regional president for Jammu and Kashmir.

Pakistan probably would like to divide up Kashmir from the rest of that province – but I think they will   compromise on this. You need a mediator someone who facilitates the negotiations – makes helpful suggestions,   calls for breaks in sessions, sets deadlines for meeting targets on agreement. You and Pakistan decide what level you want the mediator to be at. But it is a criticism from me that in the past India has rejected outside help. There are no other examples [I think] in the world where there was not facilitation for peace talks. Changing the borders can be done to a small scale for both your sides Pakistan [proper] and India [proper]. A part of the peace plan would involve the elimination of nuclear weapons here. I will then need you to work too on elimination of nuclear weapons. I want you to know nuclear weapons are evil. It is my plan to start a cascade effect getting nuclear nation after nuclear nation giving up nuclear weapons. Some day there is going to be a war somewhere in the world and it is going to involve nuclear weapons which could be disastrous for the planets existence. A war like this would escalate and escalate until nuclear weapons are used. I need your help in saving the planet.

I think of Gandhi – he refused to make differences between Muslims and Hindus. So you have two objectives peace and the elimination of nuclear weapons in the world. The pressure is on you to make peace. If you like you can email me back and give me feedback on what you think of these ideas.

Sincerely

Paul Armstrong

P.S. One day there will be no more wars on this planet</p>

PAKISTAN - INTERNAL

Purpose : To end all terrorism in Pakistan within a few years permanently.

Strategy : Using a campaign of negotiations which will provide new ways of empowering people; employ strategies for negotiating with terrorists. Campaign against terrorism in the media - providing economic improvements. I will depend on the Saudi King Abdullah Bin Abdulaziz Al Saud to work on the ideas I have given him - to work with local groups : Media / politicians / government / terrorists to bring peace to Pakistan

KEYWORDS

"Mr. Farooq H. Naek" "Terrorism" "Islam" "Peace" "PMLN Party" "Feuds" "Corruption" "Women's Rights" "Prime Minister Yusuf Gilani" "Prisoners" "The Koran" "Mr. Nawaz Sharif" "President Pervez Musharraf" "Asif Ali Zardari" "Bilawal Zardari" "Judiciary" "PPP Party" "Benazir Bhutto" "Imran Khan" "Saudi King Abdullah Bin Abdulaziz Al Saud" "Sunni - Shia - Christian Relations" "FATA / Khyber-Pakhtunkhwa Province Areas"

#7 28/06/2013 PAUL ARMSTRONG - PEACE IN PAKISTAN - TO SAUDI KING ABDULLAH

28/06/2013

TO SAUDI KING ABDULLAH BIN ABDULAZIZ AL SAUD

Dear Ambassador,

Please can you pass the following on to King Abdullah. I need his help. I need his help in bringing peace to Pakistan a country that is plagued with terrorism. I am going to be sending him emails with ideas and information on how to negotiate with terrorism | how to fight terrorism. It is his job to use these ideas personally and work with ALL the relevant people in Pakistan – terrorists / politicians / media / government to end ALL terrorism in that country. This is my last email to you. I also enclose all my previous correspondence to you on this matter. If King Abudullah finds my ideas helpful and intends to use them ask him to write back to me.

God Bless You / Allah Bless You

ISSUES

- Shi'a / Sunni / Christian Relations
- Kashmir / Afghanistan
- Islamism / State Relations / Anti-west
- State involvement in supporting terrorism

NOTES

- Lashkar-i-Jhangvi [LJ]
  - Sunni Terrorist group

- o LJ is an al-Qaeda affiliate
- o One of their leaders is Malik Ishak - Released from prison in 2011 | Jailed in 1997
- o Originally the armed wing of SSP it has morphed into the collective armed wing of various deobandi terrorist groups
- o Offshoot of Sipah-i-Sahaba Pakistan [SSP]
- o In late 1990's the organisation joined the conflict in Kashmir and received training and expertise from Deobandi terrorist groups particularly Harkat-ul-Jihad-al-Islam and Jaysh-i-Muhammad
- o By getting involved in the Kashmir dispute they gained some favour with the Pakistani military
- o Splinter group of the LJ - Lashkar-i-Jhangvi al-Alami

- Sipah-i-Sahaba Pakistan [SSP]
  - o A political party - Anti-Shi'a
  - o Leader executed in 1990 by suspected Shi'a insurgents
  - o Party banned in 2002 for links to militancy

- Sipah-i-Muhammad - Shi'a terrorist group
  - o Offshoot of the political party Tehriq Nifaz-e-Fiqa Jafria [TNFJ]

- Tehriq-e-Taliban Pakistan [TTP]
  - o Sunni terrorist group
  - o Led by Hakimullah Mehsud
  - o Since 2007 the Taliban have been targeting JUI-F some believe over rumours that their leader Rehman wss prepared to mediate between the US and Afghan Taliban
  - o Within TTP the leadership members who are Salafists consider Shi'a as infidels | The Deobandi leadership members are more tolerant and do not support attacking Shi'a unless they themselves are attacked
  - o In December 2012 TTP offered a ceasefire with the government
    - ▪ Their number of suicide attacks in 2012 declined | However their number of targeted attacks on security forces, government installations and high profile figures increased
    - ▪ Hakimullah Mehsud made the following conditions before talks could begin | 1. Pakistan should change its foreign policy and disassociate itself from the US and define its foreign policy in conformity with Islamic law 2. Pakistan's constitution should be based on Sharia
    - ▪ The TTP named three politicians as guarantors of the peace talks with the military : Former prime minister Nawaz Sharif, Maulana Fazul Rahman of Jamiat-i-Ulama-i-Islam and Munavar Hassan of Jamaat-i-Islami
    - ▪ There is some suspicion that the TTP offer of peace talks is not genuine and would be used to regroup and rearm

- Tehriq-i-Taliban Islami Pakistan [TTIP]
  - Fazal Saeed Zanimusht defected from TTP at the end of June 2011 to form a new organisation TTIP
  - Saeed gets his support from the Sunni sect in the Kurram Agency – tribes
  - Saeed defected as he opposed suicide attacks | attacks on civilians and the army. He also was angry at the TTP for not sticking to the Murree Agreement for the Kurram Agency which was renewed in February 2011 a peace agreement between Sunni and Shi'a in the region.
- Jamiat-i-Ulama-i-Islam-Fazlur [JUI-F]
  - Largest religious party in Pakistan [Sunni]
  - Links to Taliban
  - Leader - Maulana Fazlur Rehma
  - Some leaders broke off from it in disagreements over sectarianism and violence in 1980's and 1990's for form militant organisations such as
  - Sipah-i-Sahaba Pakistan [SSP] | Harkat-ul-Mujahidin [HuM] | Jaysh-i-Muhammad [JM]
  - Splinter groups such as [JUI-S] - formed by Maulana Samiul Haq
  - [JUI-N] formed by hard-core pro-Taliban leaders for JUI-F in Balochistan in 2008 general elections - They complained that JUI-F had stopped preaching jihad and supporting the Afghan Taliban - Led by Maulana Asmatullah
- Difa-e-Pakitan Council [DPC] [Defence of Pakistan Council]
  - An alliance of religious parties
  - Led by Jama'at-ul-Da'wa [JUD] - which is a front group for Lashkar-i-Tayyiba
  - Opposes strengthening of ties with India and US / US operations in Afghanistan / US drone aF\ttacks / And granting most favoured trading status to India
- Hizb al-Tahrir [HT]
  - Wants to establish an Islamic state through Da'wa and preaching rather than violence
  - Headquarters probably in the UK | present in more than 40 countries
  - Does not support participation in democratic political systems
  - HT spokesman in Pakistan is Naveed Butt
  - Imitaz Malik considered underground leader of HT in Pakistan
  - HT distributes pamphlets, holds conferences, seminars and religious lectures | pursues da'wa activities and propagates HT ideology on an individual basis
  - HT supports a strategy called "nusra" which means it could support a coup d'etat by an armed force if that force is pursuing an Islamic agenda
- Jaysh-i-Muhammad [JM]
  - Led by Masoud Azhar
  - They are a Kashmiri oriented jihadist group?,
  - The target India and other Muslim sects

- In 2003 Masoud expelled a dozen ranking members for targeting western and Christian targets in Pakistan | This resulted in a schism within the group with members leaving to form Jamaat-ul-Furqan [JuF]
- JuF constitutes part of the Punjabi Taliban

- Harkat-ul-Mujahidin [HuM]
  - Targets Kashmir | experienced a fissure when members left to form [HuMA] - Harkat-ul-Mujahidin al-Alami

- Lashkar-i-Tayyiba [LT / LeT]
  - Targets Kashmir - involved in the Mumbai attacks in India 2008
  - Has experienced fissures over its support of the Pakistani government
  - LT - Targets India and western interests there
  - Has provided a small amount of support to other terrorist groups such as Al-Qaeda and Pakistani Taliban - safe haven | reconnaissance | false papers
  - Pakistan military has occasionally targeted the organisation
  - The state has some influence over the organisation
  - LT has provided training to individuals who have then gone on to join other terrorist groups
  - LT has networks in Europe, UK, Middle East and US
  - LT is the armed wing of JuD

- Jama'at-ul-Da'wa [JuD]
  - JuD and LT are likely the same even though they are viewed as separate entities
  - JuD leader is Hafiz Saeed
  - The JuD played a major role in aiding the victims of Pakistans 2005 earthquake
  - The JuD is considered the best organised Islamic charity in South Asia

- Lashkars
  - These are tribal militias in the Khyber-Paktunkhwa Province and FATA areas that are armed by the government to deal with terrorists using their areas / trying to control their areas
  - Terrorists have killed hundreds of tribal leaders through assassinations and suicide attacks

- NACTA – National Counterterrorism Authority

- Punjabi Taliban Network
  - Lacks and organisation or command structure and acts as a loose network of elements from distinct militant groups
  - Members such as the LJ, SSP AND JM are the major groups in the Punjabi Taliban

- These three organisations do not refer to all members of these organisations but only refers to individuals or factions who shifted to FATA or collaborate with the TTP or other militant groups in the tribal areas
- Most of the groups are Salafist and Sunni in origin

RELIGIOUS ARGUMENTS

- Suicide Bombings
  - Ibn Taymiyya - His work "A principle regarding plunging into the enemy, and is it permitted" has been used as a source to justify suicide bombings but his writings repeatedly refer to an act where an individual or small number of people "plunge themselves" into battle against enemy combatants knowing they may die : note here The Enemy In This Case Is Armed!
  - In his work Ibn Taymiyya states that Muslim and non-Muslim non-combatants must not be harmed
  - Terrorists have isolated selected extracts of Ibn Taymiyya's statements
  - Sacrificing oneself according to Taymiyya must be in an actual battle and not in civilian situations
  - Ibn Taymiyya also states "And God, the sublime, tries the believers in self-devotion to the point of being killed for the sake of God and the love of his messenger. And so, if they are killed they are martyrs (Shuhada), and if they live they are happy - Clearly Taymiyya sees the possibility of the person coming out alive even when there is a risk of martyrdom something not possible in a suicide mission
- Correcting Misperceptions with the Koran
- Islam is a religion of peace – In the Koran it states :
- "And if they incline to peace, then incline to it and trust in Allah; Surely he is the hearing, the knowing" [Holy Koran 8:61]
- Mohammed has said : "Those who do not love his fellow mankind, Allah does not love him"
- Mohammed has stated – In sharing the message of Islam with others Muslims are only required to share the message, not to force others to accept Islam
- "There is no compulsion in religion"
- "And if your lord had pleased, surely all those who are in the earth would have believed, all of them; Will you then force men till they become believers?" [Holy Koran 10:99]
- "And our duty is only to proclaim the clear message" [Holy Koran 36:17]

- Islam allows Muslims and non-Muslims to live together – And Muslims are encouraged to perform good deeds to non-Muslims :
- "Allah does not forbid you respecting those who have not made war against you on account of (your) religion, and have not driven you forth from your homes, that you show them kindness and deal with them justly; surely Allah loves the doers of justice" [Holy Koran 64:8]
- Islam does not have to be at war with the rest of the world [non-believers] The concept of Dar al-Islam and Dar al-Harb cannot be found anywhere in the Koran or the Sunnah – it was developed centuries later by Muslim jurists.

- In Mohammed's time he only declared war against the Roman and Persian empires after they executed his messengers and missionaries to them and acted with hostility towards Islam. However he never called for war against Abyssinia – This country – A Christian country received refugees from Medina whom Mohammed had sent during the persecution of Muslims during the Medina period. The king of Abyssinia treated his guests well. The Muslims stayed in his country as guests until six years after the setting up of the Islamic state in Medina. Good relations between the two countries continued and the King of Abyssinia recognised the Islamic state. Mohammed never made any attempts to force religion on the country or to demand any kind of tax.
- Verses in the Koran calling for war against non-believers must be taken into context – They were made during a time in the Prophets life when his followers were coming under sustained attack from other Arab tribes – who were very hostile to him. They repeatedly violated the treaties they made with him. It is in this context that the following verses were made.
- "Fight those who do not believe in Allah, nor in the latter day, nor do they prohibit what Allah and his messenger have prohibited, nor follow the religion of truth, out of those who have been given the book, until they pay the tax in acknowledgment to superiority and they are in a state of subjection" [Holy Koran 9:29]
- O, Prophet! Strive hard against the unbelievers and the hypocrites and be unyielding to them; and their abode is hell and evil is their destination" [Holy Koran 9:73]
- "Fight them, Allah will punish them by your hands and bring them to disgrace, and assist you against them and heal they hearts of a believing people" [Holy Koran 9:14]

#6 18/06/2013 PAUL ARMSTRONG - PEACE IN PAKISTAN - TO SAUDI KING ABDULLAH

18/06/2013
TO SAUDI KING ABDULLAH BIN ABDULAZIZ AL SAUD

Dear Ambassador,
Please can you pass the following on to King Abdullah. I need his help. I need his help in bringing peace to Pakistan a country that is plagued with terrorism. I am going to be sending him emails with ideas and information on how to negotiate with terrorism | how to fight terrorism. It is his job to use these ideas personally and work with ALL the relevant people in Pakistan – terrorists / politicians / media / government to end ALL terrorism in that country. This is my sixth email I will be sending him another one on this matter. I also enclose all my previous correspondence to you on this matter.
  God Bless You / Allah Bless You

SUNNI – SHIA – CHRISTIAN RELATIONS
INTOLERANCE

- # Show what harm sectarian speeches and literature have caused in people's lives

- People who provoke sectarianism are a small minority and should be singled out
- People should talk about intolerance

TALKING ABOUT ISLAM

- The writings of acclaimed figures of various schools of thought should be made available to the maximum number of people – Broaden people's worldview
- Promote the writings of respected writers on controversial issues

- Talk about how various different sects of Islam is treated in other countries
- Debates between important personalities of diverse opinions should be made public so that people may get a positive message and extremism may be reduced
- More cooperation between religious seminaries and international religious universities

ACTIONS

- # Shia's and Sunnis going to each other's funerals and mourning together

- Getting Sunni /Shi'a leaders of other countries to intervene with their respective Sunni / Shi'a sects in Pakistan to choose peace
- If you are a minority join parties that are non-sectarian

- # Work with human-rights groups if you suffer from discrimination as a minority

- Get the President other politicians to acknowledge contributions made by individuals of minority groups to the formation; development and prosperity of Pakistan
- Create a legal agency to represent your minority
- With a legal defence fund to help members of your community – Each individual in the community contributes one rupee per year to the fund [This would add up to a lot]
- With an Educational aid fund for promising youths from your group - Each individual in the community contributes one rupee per year to the fund [This would add up to a lot]

8/06/2013

TO SAUDI KING ABDULLAH BIN ABDULAZIZ AL SAUD

Dear Ambassador,

Please can you pass the following on to King Abdullah. I need his help. I need his help in bringing peace to Pakistan a country that is plagued with terrorism. I am going to be sending him emails with ideas and information on how to negotiate with terrorism | how to fight terrorism. It is his job to use these ideas personally and work with ALL the relevant people in Pakistan – terrorists / politicians / media / government to end ALL terrorism in that country. This is my fifth email I will be sending him another two on this matter. I also enclose all my previous correspondence to you on this matter.

God Bless You / Allah Bless You

GOVERNMENT ACTIONS

ADMINISTRATION

- A terrorism court

- A high commissioner for peace in Pakistan / government committee for mediation with terrorist

- An Islamic Assembly [Parliament] alongside real parliament with limited powers – Have to be an Imam to be in the assembly

  o Areas of influence would include :
  - Charitable acts
  - Dealing with corruption
  - Dealing with religious education
  - Relations with other Muslim countries [some powers here]
  - Can appoint religious judges
  - Create Sharia laws - These laws must go to a referendum in each state where you want to enact them
  - Supervise / finance pilgrimages to Mecca
  - Finance the building of mosques and Islamic training colleges
  - Can have ministers in the federal government in areas such as education / religious affairs

POLITICAL

- Religious groups can nominate people for election to local mayor
- Religious groups [if they become a religious group] can submit laws for parliament

GOOD WORKS

- Financial compensation for those who have been tortured or detained without charge

- Repair / Improve on the Lal Masjid Mosque [which was stormed by the military in July 2007] which caused many Punjabi militants to target the state

- Government handing out alms during Ramadan

#4 29/05/2013 PAUL ARMSTRONG - PEACE IN PAKISTAN - TO SAUDI KING ABDULLAH

29/05/2013

TO SAUDI KING ABDULLAH BIN ABDULAZIZ AL SAUD

Dear Ambassador,

Please can you pass the following on to King Abdullah. I need his help. I need his help in bringing peace to Pakistan a country that is plagued with terrorism. I am going to be sending him emails with ideas and information on how to negotiate with terrorism | how to fight terrorism. It is his job to use these ideas personally and work with ALL the relevant people in Pakistan – terrorists / politicians / media / government to end ALL terrorism in that country. This is my fourth email I will be sending him another three on this matter. I also enclose all my previous correspondence to you on this matter.

God Bless You / Allah Bless You

WHEN TALKING TO TERRORISTS

RELIGION

- Make the point - There are many people in the religious community who would oppose what you say : people who have knowledge of all of the Koran and not "selected extracts"

- It does not say anywhere in the Koran that democracy is a crime

- Talk to terrorists and say "Islam allows you to change positions – you can choose peace. Mohammed did not always support violence. The

Koran provides examples of his pragmatism. Muslim scholars have changed positions over time to deal with the situations they were in."

- Everyone seems to be able to issue a fatwa - those issuing fatwas should have credentials!

EMOTIONAL ISSUES

- Talk about their families - to attackers - they can't live with this violence
- You have turned your back on many former friends in joining Jihad – this is a terrible loss
- Many of you are also becoming involved in criminal activities such as kidnapping / the drugs trade to finance your campaign which is not sanctioned by Islam
- A lot of religious clerics and tribal leaders and politicians have been prepared to die for their beliefs at your hands. This shows considerable courage. Are they martyrs?
- Most of your victims are civilians

REALISATIONS

- Not everyone in the west supports Iraq / Israel - make terrorists aware of this
- You are not going to have a single ruler who will rule over all Muslims – There are too many differences between you - Language / religious sect / climate / attitudes / customs – Uniting all Muslims in a single Umma would require the shedding of an enormous amount of bloodshed
- Negotiators : Acknowledge mistakes made to Muslims in the past
- Tell them – "You are not the first group in Islamic history to accuse all other Muslim sects outside of yourself of being heretics"

NEGOTIATIONS

- Leaders who choose peace must emphasise to their followers that they too have suffered and they are committed Muslims
- Socialise terrorists - meeting lots of people - ministers / politicians / international figures / religious figures / human rights activists - All talking about peace!

- Negotiators on all sides - eat together / pray together - get to know each other : This will improve relations

- Negotiators : When you meet each side - provide other side with summary of discussion along with your own "helpful" commentary of discussion

- Someone to take each side during negotiations - advise them and give them feedback [but they do not take part in the negotiations themselves

- Get an expert who has dealt with these kinds of issues before to talk to the two parties in the negotiations - provide their experiences

- Get former terrorists groups elsewhere who have given up violence to talk to them such as AIS - Islamic Salvation Army - Algeria / MB - Muslim Brotherhood / IG - Islamic Group / Jama'ah Islamiya - Egypt

- Access by government to rebel / terrorist leadership to deal with violations of ceasefire during ceasefire / peace implementation

- Introduce a "discussion document" to give people a basis for negotiations

#3 19/05/2013 PAUL ARMSTRONG - PEACE IN PAKISTAN - TO SAUDI KING ABDULLAH

19/05/2013
TO SAUDI KING ABDULLAH BIN ABDULAZIZ AL SAUD

Dear Ambassador,

Please can you pass the following on to King Abdullah. I need his help. I need his help in bringing peace to Pakistan a country that is plagued with terrorism. I am going to be sending him emails with ideas and information on how to negotiate with terrorism | how to fight terrorism. It is his job to use these ideas personally and work with ALL the relevant people in Pakistan – terrorists / politicians / media / government to end ALL terrorism in that country. This is my third email I will be sending him another four on this matter. I also enclose all my previous correspondence to you on this matter.

  God Bless You / Allah Bless You

PRISONERS

PEACE IDEAS

- Talk to terrorist prisoners in prison to get them to call for a ceasefire - Stress to them 1. There is a purpose to a ceasefire 2. Peace talks will make real progress. 3. They do have capable negotiators on their side
- Get religious scholars to go into prisons - Talk to terrorists : Reinterpret the Koran / debate with them
- Terrorists in prison being confronted by victim's relatives
- House arrest for leaders of religious terrorist groups during negotiations [easing sanctions]
- No criminal record for prisoners upon release if they renounce violence – making it easier for them to get a job
- Negotiate for peace with terrorist leaders in prison
- Prisoners not released immediately following peace agreement but allowed to work outside the prison while serving a small remainder sentence [lay the foundation for life after release] Conditions : Must express genuine remorse for their actions | Sever their links with the terrorist organisation | make full confession of crimes they have been involved in :- including crimes they have not been convicted of [will not be charged for the latter] | Recognition of the suffering you have caused | Terrorists can surrender to the government to participate in the scheme to end their lives as terrorists and only serve a small sentence

WINNING TERRORISTS OVER

- Bring prisoners to prisons close to where their relatives are
- Getting clerics to visit terrorists in prison and then have them visit their families to inform them about their situation - "Building Up A Relationship"
- Getting the family involved is very important in rehabilitating terrorists
- Make sure families of detainees have a source of income so they do not rely on terrorist networks
- Prison officers praying with Muslim terrorist prisoners – Win them over
- Allow a foreign government / or the Pakistan government to pay for the legal costs of terrorist trials

MAKING AMENDS

- Terrorists must pay back society when they are released from prison / make a contribution to society for a certain period of time

#2 9/05/2013 PAUL ARMSTRONG - PEACE IN PAKISTAN - TO SAUDI KING ABDULLAH

9/05/2013

TO SAUDI KING ABDULLAH BIN ABDULAZIZ AL SAUD

Dear Ambassador,

Please can you pass the following on to King Abdullah. I need his help. I need his help in bringing peace to Pakistan a country that is plagued with terrorism. I am going to be sending him emails with ideas and information on how to negotiate with terrorism | how to fight terrorism. It is his job to use these ideas personally and work with ALL the relevant people in Pakistan – terrorists / politicians / media / government to end ALL terrorism in that country. This is my second email I will be sending him another five on this matter. I also enclose all my previous correspondence to you on this matter.

 God Bless You / Allah Bless You

FATA / KHYBER-PAKTUNKHWA PROVINCE AREAS

PEACE IDEAS

- Refer to previous peace agreements in the FATA areas
- Condition to terrorists during ceasefire and peace
- Allow access by NGO's [at least Pakistani NGO's] to FATA / Khyber-Pakhtunkhwa Province areas
- Freedom of movement for police and military in FATA and Khyber-Pakhtunkhwa Province areas
- Terrorist groups meet with a grand-jirga [council of tribal elders from all tribes] for negotiations – They risk losing the support of the locals if they reject its outcome [militants have a habit of breaking agreements with the government]
- UN / NGO radio stations in tense provinces such as FATA / Khyber-Pakhtunkhwa Province – programming - peace and reconciliation, culture, religion, making people aware of extremism

FREE MOVEMENT

- Allowing exchanges of population on both sides of the Afghan-Pak border to achieve common ground on dealing with terrorism – holding Jirga's
- If you can get rid of the tolls and allow free movement of goods and people in out and through the region this will encourage business

SERVICES

- Set up religious courts in the FATA areas and Khyber-Pakhtunkhwa Province areas - Take away Taliban's influence (but more moderate than them)
- An endowment board in FATA / Khyber-Pakhtunkhwa Province areas with substantial funding
- Military bases in FATA providing healthcare facilities
- Adult education – literacy / vocational skills in the evenings at mosques
- Funding religious practices / ceremonies in tense areas as a means of appeasement
- Legal aid for vulnerable groups in Khyber-Pakhtunkhwa Province and FATA

ADMINISTRATION

- A key point here the tribes in these regions will only respect you if you are strong
- Local Civil Liaison Officers in the army to communicate with locals in FATA
- A minister for tribal areas
- Amalgamate FATA and NWPF areas into one province – Regularise its status as an electoral province so political parties can compete there – Get rid of the political agent / tribal Malik

ECONOMIC MEASURES

- The army should seek out quick-impact projects to implement and win over the local population
- Set up registration and training centres [relevant/needed skills] inside FATA for youths seeking employment in the middle east – Remittances from people working abroad can have a big impact on the economy and well-being of locals
- Under a special amnesty rule, legalise registration of all smuggled vehicles in FATA so they can be used legally for transport in FATA and Pakistan proper

- Linking large cities in Pakistan with areas in FATA / Khyber-Pakhtunkhwa Province for development
- Providing basic services is very important - A local/visiting doctor | A local ombudsman to adjudicate in minor matters | a basic health centre | a small primary school even if there are very few teachers | A market for selling local produce : Some of these are things that the Taliban have done in the past [a reason why they won over people in areas they used to control]
- Providing them with an income is crucial to winning them over

#1 29/04/2013 PAUL ARMSTRONG - PEACE IN PAKISTAN - TO SAUDI KING ABDULLAH

29/04/2013
TO SAUDI KING ABDULLAH BIN ABDULAZIZ AL SAUD

Dear Ambassador,

Please can you pass the following on to King Abdullah. I need his help. I need his help in bringing peace to Pakistan a country that is plagued with terrorism. I am going to be sending him emails with ideas and information on how to negotiate with terrorism | how to fight terrorism. It is his job to use these ideas personally and work with ALL the relevant people in Pakistan – terrorists / politicians / media / government to end ALL terrorism in that country. I will be sending him seven emails on this matter. This is the first.

PEACE IDEAS

PEACE IDEAS

- A public ceremony for the peace agreement [garnering publicity for the terrorists movement]
- Permitting the FBI to work in your country
- Allow them to have media outlets [provided they promote Islam as a religion of peace]
- Allow terrorists to get their manifesto / core ideology published in full in national newspapers in return for committing to a ceasefire
- Admit you were part of an organisation to receive amnesty

NGO'S / WOMEN'S RIGHTS

- Former members of terrorist groups who have given up violence setting up a charitable foundation [including those released from prison who have renounced violence]

- Keep distance from government - More likely to be successful in influencing the community if you do
- Use former extremists to gain credibility within the community especially among young Muslims
- Propagate ideology opposing extremism and violence [Former terrorists know exactly how extremists think more than anyone else]
- Work in the community
- Strengthen the role women can play in their communities – fund women's networks / women's groups. Encourage them to engage young people
- Tell the terrorist group : a reason to educate women is so they can teach their children

ENGAGING PEOPLE

- Engage in debate in the media forums where jihadists target recruits – [people with knowledge of the Koran / former extremists] Don't shut these sites down because they will just start up somewhere else
- Hold debates using Imams on issues relating to Islam, human rights, jihad, terrorism and extremism - In madrassas / mosques /community centres around the country for the public or selected groups : young / unemployed / other imams / women
- Cultural exchanges between Pakistan and US – in areas of Art, Literature, Music, Media, Sport. Expositions in each country with both sides in each exposition. This is even more important than the current strategy of propaganda engaged in by the US such as the US sponsored satellite station Al-Hurra. This will help end hostility with the west.
- Teach Muslims – You must reach out to more than just your own people – Be Concerned for all parts of the world : Muslim and Non-Muslim
- If you want to win people over you have to address their grievances – dealing with persecution of minorities / dealing with corruption [being forced to pay bribes] / access to speedy justice | the law / access to a fair un-corrupt police / receiving full government funding
- Encourage them to get involved in issues other than religion such as human rights / education / women's rights / corruption

FIGHTING TERRORISM

- Victims of terrorism – go into the schools talk about their experiences of terrorism on themselves and their communities whether Christian / Sunni / Shi'a – to schoolchildren | including the madrassas

- Victims – Tell terrorists "I forgive you" : An organisation to arrange visits for victims to meet terrorists in prison. Terrorists are taught to hate you and to hear someone say this may change them profoundly.

- Martyrs - People who have been killed by terrorists who were good people / people who were doing good works in society : highlight them – spread literature about them [newspapers / books / leaflets / internet] [say who killed them]

- Former terrorists publishing articles / leaflets / books in favour of peace / against extremism / criticising active terrorist groups [can use former terrorists from other countries]

- Airing confessions of militants and relatives of wanted men - to rally public against radicals

- Highlight the illegal/criminal activities terrorists are engaged in – in the media [re: fundraising etc.]

- Media campaign against terrorism - graphic imagery of victims : those killed / those injured / destruction caused – Do this in newspapers and TV – Media will have to forego ethical guidelines/restrictions

- 1. Publicise surrenders of militants on television regularly

- 2. Broadcast interviews with prisoners praising their treatment in prison

- 1. And 2. Have the effect of stemming new recruits to terrorist organisations

- Public calls for an end to violence by religious groups from other countries

- On-going training for imams - covering how to fight extremist ideologies and prevent takeovers of their mosques by extremists

- If moderate clerics want to win support away from extremists they must be seen prepared to criticize the government and also western influences [this is what extremists do]. They can still praise what is good and call for peace and moderation

FINANCIAL ISSUES

- An international donor's conference for FATA / KHYBER-PAKTUNKHWA PROVINCE in return for peace by all parties
- International community makes financial donations to moderate Muslim networks in Pakistan to assist their social services to those most in need such as the ASJ [Ahl as-Sunnah wa'l Jama'ah] – drawing support away from extremists who use social services to the poor to gain recruits and support
- Government pays a small monetary donation to each family for sending their children to school each week

ADMINISTRATION

- Form a coalition government in the regions based on the system used in Northern Ireland where all parties are represented
- Concession in negotiations with terrorists. Can appoint an Imam as head of a province / region / city / area selected by a council comprised of religious leaders OR key figures in society who have been democratically elected
- Each region / village / city votes on whether it wishes to be ruled by sharia law. They can also vote to reverse this. It is up to the people themselves to decide what they want
- Terrorists who commit to peace – You can be in regional government immediately until elections with others
- Allowing foreign country's governments to talk with political parties, civil society - could help them feel included, pacify religious parties
- Regional body to fight terrorism - Iran / Afghanistan / Pakistan
- A civil forum panel of NGO's, civil society, human rights organisations etc. Encourage this in other Muslim countries – civil forum panels from each country would meet with each other and work in parallel with the Arab League – meet at the same time and in the same country as Arab League summits
- Religious groups have access to the Prime Minister / President
- A co-president position for the largest group in the regional parliament
- Offer them a place in government including the judiciary

SRI LANKA

Purpose : To improve the rights of the minority Tamils in Sri Lanka

Strategy : To make Tamils feel free even if they are not actually free. Reiterate Tamils original goals and try to fulfill them.

<u>KEYWORDS</u>

"Army Hospitals" "Peace Agreement" "Federal Constitution" "President Mukherjee" "Prime Minister Ranil" "Tamils" "Sinhalese" "Digital Record Of Land Ownership" "International Corruption Court"

#3 PAUL ARMSTRONG - PEACE WITH TAMILS IN SRI LANKA

14/07/2015

TO INDIAN GOVERNMENT

Dear Ambassador,

Dear President Mukherjee,

Please can you pass these ideas on to the Sri lankan government and if you think it is wise host negotiations between both sides. I also include all my previous emails to you.

- Former LTTE members showing the graves of lost ones – a body set up to coordinate with these
- members
- A teachers college for Tamils
- I can't make Tamils free – but you can make them feel free
- Army hospitals
- University students working on charity projects – as part of their curriculum – compulsory
- Peace agreement presented to the media – statements made without any questioning by media present
- Each ministry can appoint their own civil service at higher levels
- Apologise for past mistreatments both sides do this
- Allow NGO's into Tamil areas
- Incentives to Tamil communities for them contributing members to the Sri Lankan army – at present only 1% of the army are Tamils
- Government support cultural events of minorities – Tamils and Muslims
- Decentralise government ministries throughout the regions

- A common points system for entry into third level colleges; Aptitude tests can be used for some courses to improve numbers of minorities in colleges
- Allow political parties to have branches in universities – host debates between groups
- International schools
- Go to Tamil areas to host secret negotiations – [A confidence building measure]
- Include people from previous negotiations into negotiating team
- A friend's of peace organisation – wear a t-shirt / jacket with this logo on it
- Tamils and Government publishing their initial positions on the negotiations<
- A merger of Tamil regions
- A regional and a national parliament – Tamils can have the same representatives in both
- UNESCO drawing up educational curriculum
- OHCHR drawing up a bill of human rights for all of Sri Lanka
- Veto powers for regional assemblies
- Change the disputed wording of "homeland" to "people's administrative region"
- Reiterate to Tamils that your initial goals were a federal constitution and parity of respect in the status of national languages
- President / Prime Minister / Politicians visiting refugee camps [Tamil]
- A share of profits of mineral companies in Tamil regions

#2 PAUL ARMSTRONG - PEACE WITH TAMILS IN SRI LANKA

13/07/2015

TO INDIAN GOVERNMENT

Dear Ambassador,

Dear President Mukherjee,

Please can you pass the following on to the Sri Lankan government.

Dear Prime Minister Ranil

The first thing you need to do is improve the lives of Tamils. They are suffering right now as a legacy of the war. I believe that nobody wants war any more - neither you nor the Tamils. Majorities [Sinhalese]must be kind and just to minorities. What I am calling on you is to increase the rights of Tamils - of your own free will. I have a number of ideas which I hope the Indian government will pass on to you. You were wrong in the past of your treatment of Tamils - historically speaking - You yourselves are not responsible for the past but you are responsible for reforms now. We are all learning from each other [other countries] how to treat minorities. Basically it boils down to not freeing [creating an independent state] but making the Tamils "feel free".

#1 PAUL ARMSTRONG - PEACE WITH TAMILS IN SRI LANKA

13/07/2015

TO INDIAN GOVERNMENT

Dear Ambassador,

Dear President Mukherjee,

I need your help to bring justice and a solution to the mistreatment of Tamils in Sri Lanka. Minority rights need to be protected. My impression of Sri Lanka is that the sinhalese are not prepared to make any real concessions to the Tamils. There probably won't be another war a reason indeed for the Sri Lanka government to act. I dont' think anyone wants another war. I include some ideas for peace. Work with both sides to bring a just solution here. Thank you for taking the time to read this email.

- Replace military personnel in Tamil areas with unarmed police force
- Police commander must be visibly seen visiting police stations to ensure proper conduct and prevent corruption
- Individuals asking politicians to go with them when making a complaint
- Create a feeling of community - community eats together once a week
- A philanthropy union of rich people and rich companies
- Tamil activists to address national parliament
- A digital record of peoples ownership of land
- An international court to deal with corruption funded by South-East Asia association
- No regional parliament but ministries must be shared with Tamils on a 1:1 footing - That would be a just society. I want to stress this point more strongly than any other point. To make this
- possible you would need a cross-party government. At least one Tamil party linked with at least one Sinhalese party irrespective of their individual sizes

- Both languages in Sir Lanka made compulsory in schools
- Important leaders visiting Tamil areas
- # Wives of male politicians elected can enter parliament themselves without having to be elected
- A south-east Asia meeting of all groups - politicians / civil society / governments - All meeting at a
- conference to decide on rights for Tamiils. The goal is not to free them but make them feel more in control of their own destiny.
- LTTE prisoners - politicians visiting them to get them to call for peace and negotiations

EUROPE

Azerbaijan / Armenia

Issues

- Contested Territory
- Lack of communication between both sides
- Occupied foreign lands
- Unresolved conflict

People Involved

- Armenian Government
- Azerbaijan Government - [Azerbaijan President]
- Nagorno-Karabakh Government

Those Working For Peace

- European Partnership for the Peaceful Settlement of the Conflict over Nagorno-Karabakh
- Minsk Group

Bosnia-Herzegovina

Issues

- Divided Country Politically
- Ethnic Hostilities
- High Unemployment Rate
- Unresolved past

People Involved

- Bosnia-Herzegovina Federal Government
- Eufor
- Republic Srpska Government

Those Working For Peace

- Center For Peacebuilding
- Eufor
- Regional Peace Initiative Network
- Youth Resource Centre (YRC) Tuzla

Georgia

Issues

- Displacement of Peoples
- Russian Involvement
- Secessionism of ethnic regions

People Involved

- Abkhazia -[President Of The Republic Of Abkahzia]
- Georgian Government -[Parliament Of Georgia]
- NATO
- http://www.government.ru/eng/gov/Russian Government
- South Ossetia

Those Working For Peace

- United Nations Observer Mission In Georgia

AZERBAIJAN / ARMENIA

Purpose :To get both governments to realise that Nagorno-Karabakh must have a shared future
Strategy : Encourage the two governments to accept outside help. Make the government of
Nagorno-Karabakh realise that there has to be compromise and that what they bear a lot of
responsibility for what they choose to accept -That some things must happen. Provide the
negotiators with options to choose from re: peace ideas.

KEYWORDS

"Disputed Territory" "Nagorno-Karabakh" "Police Force" "UN" "Tax System" "Land Dispute
Resolution" "Rotating Presidency" "Own Currency" "Foreign Relations" "International Sporting
Bodies" "Local Names" "Religious Leaders"

Azerbaijan Armenia - Peace Proposal

12/10/2013

- Allow public debate on all issues relating to peace between AZ and AR in each country
- Promote learning of each other's languages and cultures
- A federal state in AZ and AR with N.K. shared as a federal state in both countries
- Examples of other peace processes to leader's e.g. Northern Ireland
- Governments not NK decide fate of NK
- Residents of NK can have joint passports and can go into either state
- Allow international travel from NK Stepanakert airport now
- NK would have a position in the UN similar to one Palestinian Authority has had in the past
- EU / US / UN would provide training in negotiation skills to politicians in AZ / AR
- Foreign Relations :
- Can have foreign relations / consulates with other countries provided AZ / AR governments are present there too
- Can work with foreign ministers of AZ / AR – have a presence in foreign missions taken by these ministers
- Can sign international agreements
- Can allow international NGO's into the region

- Can pursue agenda independent of AZ / AR in allowed areas
- For examples of autonomous regions exerting their own foreign policy – look at the example of Kurdistan Autonomous Region in Iraq
- Each side releases all foreign prisoners it has now
- A corridor would be established between NK and AR in any peace agreement
- All of NK both those parts now in AR and those parts still in AZ would be amalgamated into one province
- Newspaper journalists can publish articles in each other's papers
- Ask the question – What are your plans for the future? How do you see peace actually being achieved with both sides agreeing? How do you prepare for peace? How are you going to deal with post-settlement tensions? Look at where you are right now!
- Hostile populations
- Displaced peoples
- You haven't talked to each other a lot except at presidential level for a long time
- NGO's are not permitted to work in both countries at the same time
- "No one wants to step forward to yield to the opposite side. This persistence is thwarting any peace process
- There are people who exploited the differences between you – Politicians who played "the ethnic card"
- Acknowledge mistakes made in the past AZ towards NK and AR towards AZ
- NK can only secede if both AZ-NK and AR-NK groups both agree to this decision | There is a precedent here - other regions have been allowed to secede after a period of time by referendum - Delay is to allow for the return of refugees and to cement the peace
- Both sides should acknowledge atrocities that were committed leading up to the war and during it AND both sides should apologise for them
- Diplomatic relations now between AZ and AR
- Russian peacekeepers in NK during peace implementation
- NK can have its own international sporting bodies just like Wales/Scotland/Northern Ireland within the UK
- A common currency for AZ / AR
- NK has its own police force
- AZ / AR governments and politicians listen to other organisations / governments debating the issue of NK together at a conference [they

are just observers here] – Organisations and governments such as OSCE / Russia / US / EU / NATO / Iran / Turkey / religious leaders / business leaders / NGO's

- Point out - shared ownership of NK would allow the return of AZ refugees
- Visa free travel between AR/AZ
- PRECEDENT : The European Parliament has stated that "the resolution of the Nagorno-Karabakh conflict must include an agreement on the status of NK and that "the people of NK should be involved in the negotiations to resolve the conflict"
- DEBATE IN MEDIA / SOCIETY :
- Call for cross-regional projects in - Diplomacy / NGO level / professional level
- Youth organisations / political movements promoting peace between two countries should be funded and supported
- Stronger pressure on both AZ/AR governments to allow greater freedom for political and social activism
- The inability of AZ/AR leaders to resolve the NK problem should be expressed and criticised publically
- The OSCE should take a more active role in the negotiation process
- Research, training and educational projects and programs should be launched into the above areas
- "The conflict between the right to self-determination of Karabakh and the right to territorial integrity of AZ cannot solve the problem of NK neither precedent will work. It can only be solved if borders lose their significance; if these borders change their function fundamentally"
- Address NK's concerns over their ethnic security within shared AZ/AR country status
- In July 2010 AZ foreign minister Elmar Mammadyarov stated "not all possible diplomatic solutions have been tried. We do believe that, with some political willingness on the part of Armenia, we can create a situation where everybody wins : Armenia, us, and all the other peoples in this region"
- During negotiations the OSCE Minsk group :
- Must be prepared to criticise any party that obstructs progress rather than meet it with silence and must publically reward compromise and trust-building
- Minsk group should make the public in AZ/AR aware of its statements / proposals and the overall responses of the two conflicting parties + a calendar of past and planned high level meetings. This will encourage the two sides to negotiate better
- AZ must cease its war threats – to allow AR to make courageous decisions. In any war AZ would be seen as the aggressor.

- If NK is to share status between AZ/AR it needs security guarantees [KEY POINT]
- ## NK can have a different style of political system within shared AZ/AR – it chooses for itself the style of system it wants
- NK has to have its own security force at some level
- Lachin corridor would be patrolled by joint AZ-NK/AR security
- Assisting in cultural improvements in NK such as an Armenian-style university | Invite students from AZ to study here too
- AZ students studying in AR and vice versa – going on exchanges to each other too
- ## NK referred to as both as NK and "Artsakh State" in AZ - symbolism is important here
- Catholicos of All Armenians – Karekin II - www.armenianchurch.org - Get the religious leaders of Armenia and Azerbaijan to call for compromise between the two countries in negotiations
- Politicians from both sides meet each other / meet the president of the other side
- Support media in setting up peace-related radio programs
- NK has the right to participate in decisions that are made about it in AZ / AR
- Combined security areas [CSA's] – where joint security operations take place between AZ/AR/Russian Forces
- Confidence Building Measures :
- Cultural events involving multi-ethnic academics / religious leaders / artists
- Local business associations attracting businesspeople from different ethnicities
- Discussions involving editors from regional media outlets - ensure commitments to eliminate inflammatory rhetoric from reporting
- Foreign countries setting up "offices" in NK
- ## UN appointed members in NK government with power to remove obstructionist officials under them – For a few years
- Non-compliance with the peace agreement by either AZ/AR would see the international community recognising the other sides right to NK
- NK cannot participate in either AZ/AR sides military – It may have its own "security" police force
- Set up a South-Caucasus Educator's Network – Teachers meet and discuss current issues / develop projects / promote understanding
- The Lachin corridor linking NK to AR should be as wide as the corridor linking Nakhchivan to AZ
- AZ / AR presidents should talk to NGO sectors before elections about increasing their freedoms
- There should be an end to the ban on AZ / AR citizens travelling to each other's countries

- Religious leaders involved in the peace negotiations – appointed by the heads of their respective religions – The Catholicos of Armenian Church and the Grand Mufti in AZ
- Including NK In Negotiations - Options :
- AR keeps NK informed of negotiations | AZ discusses some issues with NK – security / the Lachin corridor etc. / Refugee returns / The style of political administration they will be allowed to use within AZ/AR / Reconstruction in NK etc.
- If you want Armenian's to support a deal you are going to have to include NK
- To AZ president – you can say NK is not an equal player in world politics but it is an equal player in conflict resolution
- Negotiations must involve more than just leaders – Precedent : Former Armenian president Levon Ter-Petrossian had to resign in 1998 after being perceived by his colleagues as having conceded too much on his own
- Reality NK is not able to survive on its own – it receives substantial financial support from Armenia and the Armenian diaspora
- An international police force for NK during peace implementation
- Set up "friends of society" groups in NK. would be composed of equal numbers of NK. Azeri's and NK. Armenians from the community each would work as a team to deal with issues such as human rights breaches, charitable assistance, hosting cross community: sporting and social events; + cross community meetings and dealing with disputes between individuals
- Publish articles from the other country's side in each others newspapers on peace – peoples desires for peace / show their good side. Let them talk about peace initiatives; both present and past. Get the inputs of the international media on past and present peace processes and publish them
- NK can print its own money [Azeri / Armenian common currency]

BOSNIA HERZEGOVINA

Purpose : To encourage all sides - Bosniak / Croat and Serb to want to live together in peace without the current tensions - get them to see each other in a more positive light.

Strategy : Provide peace ideas which can be implemented to encourage people to work for peace wherever they are whether as politicians as journalists / teachers / religious / youth. Make suggestions to alter the political structures. Provide suggestions on generating employment which can be passed on to the business community.

KEYWORDS

"Peace Education" "Religion" "Reconciliation" "Community" "Youth" "Schools" "Politics" "Urban Planning" "Media" "Employment Ideas" "Divided Societies" "Negotiations" "Peace Journalism"

PEACE PROPOSAL 2014 – 2015

2014 - 2015

TO THE GARDAI - FOR EUFOR IN BOSNIA HERZEGOVINA

TO DRAGOMIR MILOSEVIC - PAUL ARMSTRONG

20/07/2015

To Tartu Prison - Estonia - To Bosnian War Criminal - Dragomir Milosevic

Dear Sir / Madam,

This email is directed to Dragomir Milosevic former war criminal from Bosnia. I am not a journalist - but I am someone who works on peace [check my peace website at http://www.peace-implementation.info] He does not have to write back to me.

Dear Mr Dragomir,

I need your help - a lot of your help. I think you are sorry for the crimes you committed but you can do more than be sorry - you can help make things better. You have seen the horrors of war and what it can do to a person You were in a position of responsibility. I am asking you to write to a Serbian newspaper in Bosnia and in Serbia. Your letter should go something like this - That you wish you could change the past and that you want your side to apologise AND call for peace and reconciliation. I would hope that you support the Bosnian federation as it exists now. I hope this gets through to you - You are important to peace. Ask fellow prisoners from the former Yugoslavia to do the same here as you.

Sincerely

- Building satellite towns and villages for alternate ethnic groups

- Joint public meetings of Croats / Serbs / Muslims - talk about their problems to a panel of politicians

- Each community appointing leaders to engage with the other communities - hold conferences together - form a commitment to action

- Broadcast criminal trials of the ICTY on television in Bosnia

- Can write about people who have not been tried but committed crimes during the war in media - All ethnic groups can do this

- Go to each others funerals - even if the relationship is very tenuous

- Reach out - light candles for each other in Churches or Mosques simply out of sympathy that a family has lost someone AND sign your name in a book of remembrance

- Go back in groups to your home town / village - can reclaim homes / rebuild them

- Names of streets / parks / burial sites - keep the old names + repair monuments from before the war

- Joint religious masses for Muslims; Croats; Serbs - develop a format for this once a month

- Build schools next to each other | churches mosques next to each other

- Subsidised housing for minorities

- Point out that Serbs have been uprooted too

- Talk about how things used to be under Tito

- Make repairing damaged homes a priority - so more people can return home

- A single team in each city for each sport - GIVE PEOPLE SOMETHING IN COMMON WHICH THEY CAN TALK ABOUT - hosting grounds should be built in minority areas

- Parents councils for integrated schools - HAVE SOMETHING IN COMMON TO TALK ABOUT
- Artist's centres in large towns / cities where different ethnic groups can meet together HAVE SOMETHING IN COMMON TO TALK ABOUT
- Feast day meals 3-4 times a year - free food and drink for all ethnic groups in the town / village that attend
- Bosnian emigrants returning home to visit old friends
- Get advertising agencies to design emblems for army / country flag / sports teams / school uniforms and a national anthem
- Don't teach history except in university
- "TALK TO ME" logo on t-shirts / jackets
- Parents talk about friends you had with other ethnic groups to your children - leave out the history
- Dating agencies - cannot specify ethnicity - first names only
- Use statistics to promote peace - For example a survey in 2002 found that Serbs in Vukovar and Muslims in Prijedor were most open to inter-marriages with other nationalities
- Welcoming committees for new arrivals to towns / villages communities irrespective of their ethnicity
- An NGO fund 5% of taxes - NGO's are doing the most to bring about healing   - muslims may consider this their "zakat" [Muslim word for tax for the poor]
- Talk about your friends from other ethnic groups in the media - You are ambassadors for peace
- Children from different ethnic groups feel unsafe playing together - Here adults can take a role - assisting teachers / monitoring school play areas
- Introducing scouting clubs - must be inter-ethnic - get assistance from abroad to set this up - Germany / Ireland etc.
- Can have your own textbooks - a selection to choose from but common examinations

- A shared back garden with several houses from different ethnic groups on each street

- Renewing friendships over the internet - easier to see if the other side wants to renew their friendship with you too - share email addresses - avoids the risk of meeting the other physically and being rejected

- People should learn to talk about their own "personal" suffering and not the suffering of their entire group - People will discover that whatever the groups they come from;

- they have a lot in common

- People who emigrated due to mixed marriages write back to newspapers in BiH - what they would like to see happen there

- College students must spend a term working for an NGO - compulsory as part of their degree course

- Double voting for minorities

- International schools funded by the EU

- Share out jobs for ambassadors equally among ethnic groups

- Majority of social welfare payments go to communities rather than individuals

- Top 10% of high school graduates from each class - guaranteed places in BiH universities

- Minorities in government institutions - speak up for the rights of your minority

- Free meals for children up to end of secondary school and free uniforms - having uniforms encourages students to stay in schools

- In schools learn under the language used before conflict began - ethnic languages must be taught separate from schools

- A commission for employment - can visit small businesses and investigate if they are

- paying taxes

- Government funding for the poorest sections of society - this is the best way to grow economically

- Bring minorities for their region and intellectuals together in a forum to discuss overcoming racial inequalities - other ethnic groups can be observers at these forums
- Keep ethnic symbols out of the workplace / schools / city centres
- Recruitment by merit - An employment agency to ensure this rather than quotas. Encourage minorities to apply for jobs through advertising [compulsory]. Agency publishes ethnic quality levels annually
- Religion is only taught in primary schools - secondary schools must be egalitarian
- Can apply for college places in other countries
- Husbands / wives of prime ministers taking up social causes
- Companies must have certain proportion at least of each minority on board of management
- Break up BiH into smaller states - reduce chances of ethnic mobilisation
- Communities coming together to sponsor scholarships for students
- Wives of husbands who are elected can be included in parliament - without themselves having to be elected
- A single business forum for all of BiH - promote the case of a single state in economic terms
- UNESCO writing the books for education
- A single police force
- Cannot vote for your own ethnic group in politics - have to vote for someone from the other sides
- Diaspora returning to visit graves of loved ones - Typically it is those with mixed marriages that sought asylum during and after the war
- Rural assemblies - with same powers as villages / towns / cities - generally rural areas are more ethnically mixed
- Embassies hosting politicians from across the divides for meals - informal conversations - bring lots of other embassies together to create an appropriate mix
- Re-branding history - to times of peace and tolerance - such as during the socialist era
- A wall to write on - between boundaries of different ethnic groups - NGO's organise this. Tourists writing on the walls - messages of peace

- Families take on children from other ethnic groups - day holidays for them

  Women have to reach out to each other first. It has been said that the heart of a woman is compassion - Prove it. In some countries it is the women who reach out first to the other side for peace such as Somalia. It can be so for BiH. People are afraid to make the first move for fear of rejection - Be Brave here. It is going to take bravery and compassion to change BiH and women must lead first.

  Create A Single business organisation for all of BiH - They can have a division within them that supports peace projects

- Decentralise government - different ministries in different towns / cities
- Human rights groups and NGO's coming together to produce their own media publication
- NGO's lobbying journalists
- A peace journalists network
- Community media in small villages / towns - NATO sponsors this [with a sections for minorities in the area
- Universities allowing politicians / journalists to speak before assemblies from the college
- Lower the voting age for people - young people are more idealistic
- Leadership training for youths by political parties
- Youth organisations promoting issues around election time
- Have to retire from politics when over a certain age - get rid of the old block
- Allow people to visit their former homes / towns / villages in RS and BiH
- Newspapers publish articles in others languages
- Rewards for people working for peace
- Get signatures across the country for a manifesto committing the individual to work for peace in their homes / schools / workplaces and support minorities
- Politicians required to say what they have done in the past and what they intend to do
- A bigger parliament in Federal Bosnia - more chances for moderates to get elected
- Free media time for all political parties around election time
- A national peace secretariat - Harness work of politicians, trade unions, business, church, police, army

- International Political Conference in BiH
- NGO's working on peace culture recognised by Mayors of towns and cities

<u>PEACE CULTURE CONFERENCES</u>

Get the following together in conferences :

- For the establishment of education for a culture of peace : ask teachers / students
- For security : ask police
- For free flow of information : ask journalists from all media
- For measurement of democratic participation : ask politicians from mainstream and alternative parties
- For assessment of understanding, tolerance and solidarity : ask religious figures, traditional peace movement activists

- ## Rank cities / towns for their level of adherence to peace indicators

- A social forum - set goals for the city

- ## Peer groups for the Balkans - similar to AU peer council - have to reach certain social and political standards to be a member

- ## Peer groups within BiH - towns / cities / villages

- Set a vision for the future of your town / city - goals / objectives to get all groups public / CSO / Governance to work towards
- Don't teach the history of the conflict - forgetting the past is better
- School tours to other parts of RS and BiH

- ## Free fees for students attending college

- Finance cultural projects for other ethnic minorities - Create religious centres of prayer in city centre
- A street for cafes, nightclubs in the city. A cultural zone, a religious zone
- Music festivals - bring in people from abroad

- ## Open neighbourhood days - the front door house stays open all day and people can visit each other from other ethnic backgrounds

- Get rid of war memorials celebrating fighters; including in city centres - its about creating a new history
- Finance memorials for other ethnic groups
- ## Mandatory involvement of NGO's in municipal and local planning and budgeting oversight

- Celebrate each others religious holidays
- NGO's setting up meetings between people and an individual politician
- NGO's advertising in the media

- Media publishing opposing perspective on views from politicians / CSO's
  - Appointing CSO members to tempoary and permanent working bodies, commissions; boards within executive and legislative bodies
  - Encourage the development of policy / advisory groups
  - Public consultations on issues
  - Phone-in debates for all people groups to radio / tv
- Bosniac Federation talking to Serbia - make friends with them
  - A foreign news agency - tv / radio - broadcasting in BiH in local language
  - Politicians cannot own media outlets
  - Publish threats to people in the media
  - Get the BiH Diaspora to contribute to peace - Return to their former homes - meet the friends that stayed behind
  - Serbian Patriarch going to meet FBiH leaders
  - Single business associations for each city / town
  - A single womens organisation for all of Bosnia
  - Cross-party humanitarian work
  - Talk about how you would solve the problems of other cities / communities in community meetings
- Say what you think the other sides needs and fears are in community meetings
- A ceremony after a peace agreement between communities - involving gift giving
  - Flat rate in cities for bus fares
  - Aprenticeships for young people - subsidised by the state
- Relatives of a person can gain ownership of property - A simple form - no bills - while the person is still alive
  - Rebuild significant sites that were destroyed during the war rather than memorials
- Going to each others funerals [across ethnic lines] - of long lost friends / distant relatives / friends of friends
  - Integrated schooling in special schools for special skills : computing / languages / science
  - An assembly for peace and conflict NGO's in BiH - discuss ideas / work together
- A Facebook site specifically for BiH

- Peace NGO's hosting political parties for talks / negotiations eg. Fondation Hirondelle
  - A passport / visa free area for all former Yugoslav states
  - Get children to do research on ethnic problems / on ethnic diversity / on conflict issues - assistance from teachers
  - Produce media - websites / newspapers from young people on issues that matter to young people [across the ethnic lines]
  - Introduce other ethnic groups – history and culture in a positive way
  - Make young people aware of issues of social justice
  - Talk about peace in the classroom - what is/has been done about it in Bosnia; Give a history of peace in the world - what causes war/what brings peace. Give examples. Teach peace as a subject
- Get young children to use art to promote peace in schools
  - A course in peace education for teachers during their training / as a refresher course
- School-children - write about good things you know about people/children from other ethnic groups | positive experiences you have had with people from other ethnic groups you have encountered as a project
  - Religious leaders should speak up for other minorities in the community – this is a priority - regularly
- Call people from other ethnic groups to come back
- Get people to speak at churches / Mosques - good people on issues across the ethnic divide
  - Religious groups can attend meetings of parliamentary committees / local council meetings as observers
  - Religious groups can submit laws to parliament
  - Do something for free in your life maybe related to your profession
  - Say good things about people from other ethnic groups at least once each day – don't spread bad gossip about them – saying good things spreads peace / bad information destroys peace – You have to actively do this!
  - Businesses partnering with peace organisations / NGO's
  - Businesses promoting these Organizations abroad
- Get the media to report positive news articles about young people
- A youth section in newspapers written by young people once a week

- Develop pen pals between youth from the different ethnic groups in Bosnia
- Provide job references for youths who attend a Youth NGO centre for a good while
- Civil Society / NGO's can run for election as parties/individuals - Stay independent
- of other parties [This should shake up the political scene in Bosnia :-)]
- A public speakers corner in communities – [use it for good] – with well known people
- Put responsibility for redevelopment of the main towns and cities in Bosnia into the hands of a cooperative of businesses – they develop the plans; They make the decisions; They do the building. Take it out of the hands of politics – there is too much division there.
- Cultural showcase of your own ethnic tradition for others to sample – food / art
- / literature
- Keep reporting an issue in the media if you want to bring about change.
- UN / NGO's talking on radio stations and in the newspapers given regular space to talk. Enhance contact between media and journalists / international media outside the country - CNN / BBC etc. will help bring the situation in Bosnia to the world stage
- Talk about people who did good things during the civil war on all sides Serbs / Croats / Muslims - show people there are good people everywhere.
- An NGO coming into schools giving talks to children on all the cultures in Bosnia; talking about peace; talking about realising what is racism and about people who are out there doing good.
- Young peoples organisations asking their local religious leaders [Muslim/catholic/orthodox] to pass on speeches they have made on issues relevant to them. They tell people what they want changed in society.
- Get youths to talk with young people in conflict societies from other parts of the world and share ideas/experiences.

- Suggest the setting up of a Peace Radio station in your country – this has been done

- successfully in other countries such as DRC by Fondation Hirondelle [www.hirondelle.org/]. You will need to contact this organisation to ask them to set up and run the radio station.

- Ask for the setting up of a peace college – where people of all ages – youth/adults can be trained in peace skills – leadership/media work/community project work/NGO formation / peacebuilding. Courses could be long and short and there would be no pre-qualification requirements to take on a course. The college could have branches outside of Sarajevo in places like Mostar and Banja Luka.

GEORGIA

Purpose : To create an international body that would coordinate links between Georgia and the de facto states of Abkahzia and South Ossetia with their involvement

Strategy : Create structures that would allow Georgia and South Ossetia and Abkhazia to work together. Include ideas for autonomy. Preserve their ethnic majority

KEYWORDS

"Citizenship" "Politics" "Information Houses" "Negotiations" "Civil Society" "Ethnicity" "Federal Structures" "PoliticalL Structures" "Language Rights" "Refugees" "Peacekeeping" "Own currency"

GEORGIA PEACE PROPOSAL

19/12/2013

CITIZENSHIP

- Abkhazia and South Ossetia can have joint passports with Russia
- A UN passport to enter Abkhazia or South Ossetia
- Abkhazia and South Ossetia can keep their own names
- South Ossetia ,Abkhazia and Georgia citizens to be issued "Status Neutral Travel Documents" for all of them :- with a general reference name such as "Caucasus Region"

POLITICS

- Political organisations in exile can take part in regional elections after peace has been achieved
- South Ossetia and Abkhazia can set up "Information Houses" in other countries
- Regional political parties would be allowed to exist
- Change Russian embassies in Abkhazia and South Ossetia to consulates
- Allow Abkhazia and South Ossetia government officials attend international conferences [non-political conferences]
- Abkhazia and South Ossetia allowed to share foreign offices with Georgia

- Allow politicians to meet outside political talks on an unofficial basis for an exchange of ideas and opinions from South Ossetia / Abkhazia and Georgia

- Russian president asking South Ossetian / Abkhaz leaders to visit Georgian capital to begin talks | Georgian leadership reciprocating by visiting Tshkinvali / Sukhumi

- Negotiators speaking before parliaments in Tbilisi / Tskhinvali / Sukhumi to present proposed peace agreement and present their reasons for the decisions made

NEGOTIATIONS

- Abkhaz society and government should not ask the question "why do western countries refuse to recognise us?" and instead should ask "what can we do to encourage the international community to change its attitude towards us?"

- International body leading Georgian region to guarantee Abkhaz status

- Negotiations between Georgia and Abkhazia to take place in a third party country. This would be welcomed by Abkhaz side – by giving it a sense of independence.

- Have plenty of international witnesses to the negotiations and to the signing of the agreement

- Civil Society from South Ossetia / Abkhazia and Georgia all included in negotiations

- A group of experts to advise each side

- Both sides should acknowledge that the other side has suffered a lot from the Abkhaz-Georgian conflict / South Ossetian-Georgian Conflict

- At peace conferences – signs with country names should be replaced with participants surnames

HIGHER INTERNATIONAL BODY RULING THE REGION

- Precedent : In 2004 president Mikheil Saakashvili stated that "Therefore, we after immediate negotiations to our Abkhazian and Ossetian friends. We are ready to discuss every model of statehood, by taking into consideration their interests for the promotion of their future development".

- International community – UN/EU/Russian Federation guides and administers [to a degree] Georgian / Abkhazian / South Ossetian region :- Federal Structures [They can appoint people to leadership – from suggested selections from South Ossetia, Abkhazia and Georgia] They also provide administrative leadership themselves.

- The principle of equal participation between South Ossetia / Abkhazia and Georgia in any new political structures is important

- A Caucasus regional body to help administer Georgia region

SOCIAL / HUMANITARIAN

- Allow Abkhaz and South Ossetian students to attend European universities
- The Georgian government continues to provide free medical assistance to people from Abkhazia and South Ossetia
- Speed up construction of crossing points at Administrative Border Line between Gali district and Georgia.
- Allow family visits between South Ossetia / Abkhazia and Georgia immediately.

- Abkhazia should allow Georgian to be taught in its schools at least in Georgian populated areas alongside Abkhazian.

- Allow international NGO's into Abkhazia and South Ossetia immediately.
- Focus on youth and educational exchanges to reduce negative stereotyping by future generations.
- Set up an EU information office in Sukhumi and Tskhinvali to liaise with civil society there.
- Abkhazia / South Ossetia NGO's can be allowed to develop links with European NGO's.

REFUGEES / ETHNICITY

- Assist in attracting ethnic Abkhazians in diaspora / settled in other countries to move / return to Abkhazia. International community provide financial assistance for this.

- All Georgian IDP's return to one region AND / OR annex part of Abkhazia containing most ethnic Georgians into Georgia proper

- Return of all refugees to South Ossetia and to Gali District of Abkhazia

- The bottom line for the Abkhaz was fear of extinction as a separate ethnic community.

PEACEKEEPING

- Russian Military bases allowed to be in Georgia proper [not Abkhazia or South Ossetia] – Georgia may still join NATO too.
- Allow peacekeepers from more CIS/ Caucasian countries into South Ossetia / Abkhazia.

Economic

- Free trade zones along part of the border zone areas between Georgia and South Ossetia / Abkhazia
- Provide incentives, such as promising aid increases to both Georgia and Abkhazia / South Ossetia if a settlement is reached
- A European style currency for Georgia/Abkhazia/South Ossetia
- Each region can print their own money

MIDDLE EAST

IRAQ

Issues :

- Effects Of Former Sanctions
- Muslim / Christian Conflict
- Shia / Sunni Conflict
- Warlords / Religious terrorists

People Involved :

- Iraq Government [Ministry Of Foreign Affairs]
- Iraq Military

Those Working For Peace :

- Civil Development Organization
- Insan Iraqi Society
- Muslim Peacemaker Teams
- Reach
- Silm Network
- Women Leadership Institute

ISIS

Issues :

- Sharia Law
- New State
- Caliphate
- Islam

People Involved :

- Syria
- Iraq
- OIC

Those Working For Peace :

- OIC

LEBANON

Issues :

- Awkward Political System
- Hezbollah
- Reconstruction of Buildings

Those Involved :

- Hezbollah
- Lebanon President
- Druze / Shia / Sunni Communities
- Lebanon Government

Those Working For Peace :

- AIE Serve
- Arab Working Group For Muslim-Christian Dialogue
- Forum For Development,, Culture And Dialogue [FDCD]
- Lebanese Foundation For Permanent Civil Peace [LFPCP]

IRAQ

Purpose : One email here is important "17/01/2012 : TO PRIME MINISTER NOURI AL MALIKI AND DEPUTY PRIME MINISTER SALEH AL MUTLAQ" This email describes how to negotiate with an insurgent / terrorist group to get them to call a ceasefire.

Strategy : Get the terrorist group to realise that their activities will no longer work - they are loosing support and now is a key moment to negotiate.

KEYWORDS

"US Invasion" "Insurgency" "Minority Rights" "PM Nouri Al Maliki" "Vice President Tariq al Hashemi" "Iraq Army" "Violence" "Ceasefires" "US Defence Secretary Robert Gates" "Iraq Foundation" "Social Dissent"

"Mr. Al-Baghdadi"

PAUL ARMSTRONG - PEACE PROPOSAL IRAQ

14/06/2014

TO IRAQ PRIME MINISTER + DEPUTY PRIME MINISTERS

To the ambassador,

Dear Sir,

I have some proposals for peace in Iraq. Please can you pass the following on to BOTH Prime Minister Nouri Al Maliki and to the Deputy Prime Ministers.

- Make public statements calling for peace
- Get the business community to talk to the rebels calling for negotiations – They may listen to them – Including the business community in rebel held areas. If you need the USA help for this ask them – but I would go no further than this with the USA. Business is business – they could offer investment in your country.
- Tell the rebels that in negotiations they can include religious figures of their choice in their negotiating team – [You Can Too]
- Suggest that talks be held in Egypt – a neutral country
- A civil society assembly to put forward ideas for negotiations [Tell the rebels you will do this]
- In negotiations a few ideas
- Suggest that Sunni areas be treated the same way Kurdistan was treated [a regional government]
- Offer to allow imams to run administrative councils in small towns and villages as part of a team

DOING GOOD WITH THE ARMY

- Give people space to air their views / complaints even if they are negative – releasing tensions can bring about healing and trust
- Get people to come to the army and ask for help - get them to discuss among themselves – come up with options and answers and then go to the army – they get their voices heard
- Reward soldiers for reducing violence in their areas
- Get the army to represent the people [their interests / concerns] not the government
- Army act as facilitators between general population and governance – connect them to the right people / insist on timely implementation

TO PRIME MINISTER NOURI AL MALIKI AND DEPUTY PRIME MINISTER SALEH AL MUTLAQ

17/01/2012
TO IRAQ PRIME MINISTER + IRAQ DEPUTY PRIME MINISTER [iraq cabinet]

Dear Sir / Madam
Please can you pass the following on to BOTH Prime Minister Nouri Al Maliki and Deputy Prime Minister Saleh Al Mutlaq. I enclose a list of ideas on a strategy for negotiating with terrorists. I hope it works!
- Acknowledge wrongs have been committed [to the insurgent group]
- [to insurgent group] Talk to the people you claim to represent – ask them for their opinions – should you negotiate
- Point out to them all terrorist movements move from violence to peace eventually
- Say to them there is a lot of work to be done – even after a ceasefire and peace
- Tell them - If you turn to peace – you can be a lobby movement for your cause – you will probably get more support – model yourself on other peaceful Islamic movements
- Point out to them – now is the best time in history to negotiate
- Ask them what progress they have achieved with violence – not a lot
- Tell them submit your ideas to the public at large
- Tell them you want more members – you are going to have to choose the path of peace
- Tell them you are going to have to talk to other groups – DIALOGUE

- Acknowledge the wrongs that have been committed [to the insurgent group]
  I know that you have some just grievances; we have committed wrongs. People have been hurt. But now we want peace. Will you talk to us. The reason you started fighting was because you perceived injustices and wanted to protest against them. Now I am telling you – you can end those injustices and achieve a just peace by talking to us.

- [to insurgent group] Talk to the people you claim to represent – ask them for their opinions – should you negotiate

  Talk to those you represent ask them what they think of the situation. Ask the people on the ground from your community do you want us to negotiate – do you want us to continue fighting. Are you tired of the suffering. Do you trust us to come up with a just settlement for you

- Point out to them all terrorist movements move from violence to peace eventually

  I wish to point out to you – History does repeat itself – all terrorist movements eventually move from fighting to pursuing peace. In the end you too will choose peace it is just a matter of when. Time and again terrorists have realised that there actions stand to succeed more if they turn from violence to peace. Yes violence gave them a voice – but it will not gain them an agreement for that they need to pursue peace.

- Say to them there is a lot of work to be done – even after a ceasefire and peace

  Even when you do choose peace – there is still a lot of work to be done. We need to rebuild this country – heal the wounds of hatred and grief. We need to reintegrate former fighters into peaceful activities. You are a part of this future.

- Tell them - If you turn to peace – you can be a lobby movement for your cause – you will probably get more support – model yourself on other peaceful Islamic movements

  If you turn to peace – you can enter politics – you will be able to talk to the media freely – you will be listened to by a greater audience. You will be heard. You will achieve progress. Please model yourself on other Islamic movements such as the Muslim brotherhood in Egypt. Who knows you may even end up in a coalition government some day.

- Point out to them – now is the best time in history to negotiate

  Now is the best time to negotiate – People are tired of the violence on all sides. There are elements of people ready to listen and negotiate on all sides –politicians have become pragmatic – they know they have to talk to you – that the fighting is only leading to a stalemate. This was not so in the past.

- Ask them what progress they have achieved with violence – not a lot

  What progress have you made using violence – Not a lot. You have been fighting for several years now. All I see is a war of attrition with neither side able to defeat the other completely. If you do not try and take the peace option what does the future hold for you - only continued strife and suffering for everyone.

- Tell them submit your ideas to the public at large

  If you choose peace – you will be given the opportunity to submit your ideas to the public at large. You will be addressing more people than you ever have before and what's more the press will not be reporting you in a hostile way instead in an open business like way. But you must choose peace for this to happen.

- Tell them - you want more members – you are going to have to choose the path of peace

You are not a large organisation – at least not directly speaking and the people are getting tired of violence – that's where the majority of people lie. If you wish to become a bigger organisation and have a real voice – if you wish to recruit more members you are going to have to choose the path of peace.

- Tell them - you are going to have to talk to other groups – DIALOGUE
  You cannot act in isolation forever – you need to broaden your base; you want other people to listen to you – you are going to have to talk to other groups – This means dialogue – To come out of this isolation you must choose peace.

ISIS

KEYWORDS

"ISIS" "Islam" "rebellion" "Syria" "Iraq"

21/05/2015 I.S.I.S. PEACE IN SYRIA / IRAQ - PAUL ARMSTRONG

21/05/2015

TO I.S.I.S. via Iran embassy [Ireland]

Dear Ambassador Javad Kachoueian,

Can you make sure this get through to the I.S.I.S.

Dear Sirs,

The first thing I want to say is you are all SUPPOSED to be brothers - Islam is a brotherhood. You are more good than Christians right now. I have seen American imperialism - not just lives lost but also peoples innocence destroyed. War is a terrible thing and there is no glory in it. I know you want to establish a caliphate - the west would fear this - I don't - If you can have a European Union of nations why not the same for Muslims. BUT to establish a caliphate now through violence would require the shedding of an enormous amount of bloodshed. Some people say destroy everything and rebuild it as it was in the past. I must point out to you that the Koran precedes and supersedes haddith and the Sunnah. Mohamed has said THERE CAN BE NO COMPULSION IN RELIGION - it is written specifically in the Koran. Sometimes I think people make claims that are not found anywhere in the Koran. There are two forces at work in life - love and fear. If you intend to instill fear in the people you rule - that creates a bad lesson. War is wrong; you will not achieve your goals. You differ from the vast majority of Muslims - Why aren't Muslims everywhere rebelling if they wanted a caliphate or a caliphate through violence - because they do not want to. I want you to know that Islam is a good religion but you are not representing a majority. The Qumran and Muhammad encourage Muslims to decide their affairs in consultation with those who will be affected by that decision. That is a good thing - please…

An idea would be to set up Shura councils in village / town and city administrations combined with an electoral parliament for the country. You won't win this war but you have pushed the issue of uniting Muslims. I am calling on you to turn to peace now. It is easy to kill someone it is not so easy to make peace. The only winners in this war are the people selling the guns. I know there are divisions between Sunnis and Shiites - that does not make me happy. A few suggestions here :

INTOLERANCE

- Show what harm sectarian speeches and literature have caused in people's lives
- People who provoke sectarianism are a small minority and should be singled out
- People should talk about intolerance

TALKING ABOUT ISLAM

- The writings of acclaimed figures of various schools of thought should be made available to the maximum number of people – Broaden people's worldview<
- Promote the writings of respected writers on controversial issues
- Talk about how various different sects of Islam is treated in other countries
- Debates between important personalities of diverse opinions should be made public so that people may get a positive message and extremism may be reduced
- More cooperation between religious seminaries and international religious universities

ACTIONS

- Shia's and Sunnis going to each other's funerals and mourning together
- Getting Sunni /Shi'a leaders of other countries to intervene with their respective Sunni / Shi'a sects in Syria to choose peace
- If you are a minority join parties that are non-sectarian
- Work with human-rights groups if you suffer from discrimination as a minority
- Get the President other politicians to acknowledge contributions made by individuals of minority groups to the formation; development and prosperity of Pakistan
- Create a legal agency to represent your minority
- With a legal defence fund to help members of your community – Each individual in the community contributes one Syrian pound per year to the fund [This would add up to a lot]
- With an Educational aid fund for promising youths from your group - Each individual in the community contributes one Syrian pound per year to the fund [This would add up to a lot]

LEBANON

Purpose : To make politics more efficient

Strategy : Using the D'Hondt Method for governance where a grand coalition of many parties is assembled. Representing people more efficiently

<u>KEYWORDS</u>

"Lebanon" D'Hondt Method" "Grand Coalition Government"

Peace In Lebanon - Paul Armstrong

Dear Ambassador,

I have a few suggestions for peace in Lebanon. You may be familiar with the "de-Hondt method" which was used in Northern Ireland. I believe it can work for Lebanon too. The de-Hondt method needs to be explained to them. Please pass the following on to the prime minister of Lebanon and work with him on implementing this new peace agreement.

Dear Mr prime minister Tammam Salam,

I enclose some ideas for a new structure of government. The following is known as the de-Hondt method.

Allocating seats ministries in government [your government would be a coalition government of most parties] is done using the following formula quot = number of votes divided by s + 1 where s is initially nought. In the first round the party with the highest vote is divided by 1 and gives them the choice of first seat. In the second round all original votes are divided by 2 and the party with the highest vote now [after dividing all parties votes by 2] gets to choose what minister they wish to have in government. In the third round the new number of quot [after divisions] is divided by 3 and the party with the highest vote now [from any of the rounds] gets to appoint the next minister. I provide a table to help you understand this method.. The de-Hondt method makes for representative government – in a grand coalition.

In this example, 230,000 voters decide the disposition of 8 seats among 4 parties. Since 8 seats are to be allocated, divide each party's total votes by 1, then by 2, 3, 4, 5, 6, 7, and 8. The 8 highest entries, marked with asterisks, range from 100,000 down to 25,000. For each, the corresponding party gets a seat.

For comparison, the "True proportion" column shows the fractional numbers of seats due, calculated in proportion to the number of votes received. (For example, 100,000/230,000 The slight favouring of the largest party over the smallest is apparent. In this example, 230,000 voters decide the disposition of 8 seats among 4 parties. Since 8 seats are to be allocated, divide each party's total votes by 1, then by 2, 3, 4, 5, 6, 7, and 8. The 8 highest entries, marked with asterisks, range from 100,000 down to 25,000. For each, the corresponding party gets a seat. For comparison, the "True proportion" column shows the fractional numbers of seats due, calculated in proportion to the number of votes received. (For example, 100,000/230,000 × 8 = 3.48)The slight favouring of the largest party over the smallest is apparent.

denominator	/1	/2	/3	/4	/5	/6	/7	/8	Seats won (*)	True proportion
Party A	**100,000***	**50,000***	**33,333***	**25,000***	20,000	16,666	14,286	12,500	4	3.48
Party B	**80,000***	**40,000***	**26,666***	20,000	16,000	13,333	11,428	10,000	3	2.78
Party C	**30,000***	15,000	10,000	7,500	6,000	5,000	4,286	3,750	1	1.04
Party D	20,000	10,000	6,666	5,000	4,000	3,333	2,857	2,500	0	0.70

Table under the creative commons license http://creativecommons.org/licenses/by-sa/3.0/

D'Hondt Method : https://en.wikipedia.org/wiki/D'Hondt_method

SOUTH AMERICA

Colombia

Issues :

- Left-Wing Terrorism
- Social Injustices
- Corruption
- Poverty
- Crime
- Drug Production
- Paramilitary Forces

People Involved :

- FARC-EP
- ELN
- Colombian Government

Those Working For Peace :

- Colombian Catholic Church
- International Community
- Colombian Government
- FARC-EP Peace Delegation 2012
- ColombiaPeace.org
- Movement For Peace In Colombia
- Colombia Peace Fund
- Justice For Colombia
- Colombia Support Network - Peace And Justice
- The Peace Village San Jose
- REDEPAZ
- INDEPAZ

COLOMBIA

Colombia - Peace Proposal

Purpose :To end terrorism. To make a more just society

Strategy : Provide avenues for FARC-EP / ELN to influence politics.Provide greater social justice for the poor. Improve policing in Colombia's cities and towns.

KEYWORDS

"Colombia" "South America" "FARC-EP" "ELN" "Social Justice" "NGO's" "Wealth Tax" "Reforms" "Land" "Negotiations" "Policing" "Participatory Budgeting"

Political

- Make compensation for wrongs done in the past – killing of politicians : FARC-EP political party during the 1990's Patriotic Union party most of whose members were slaughtered
- FARC-EP/ELN Leaders to address parliament
- ELN/FARC-EP and government to draft joint bills for submission to parliament for reforms
- FARC-EP/ELN can nominate people to judiciary system / human rights boards / government ministries [instead of taking the posts themselves]
- Allow FARC-EP / ELN publish their goals in the national media
- Broadcast civil assembly meetings in local radio and on television
- Get former members of other terrorist groups from South America to talk to FARC-EP / ELN such as former FMLN members from El Salvador
- ELN / FARC-EP acknowledge their major crimes and ask the catholic church for pardon
- Make people aware of the peace agreement – through the media / government organisations
- A congress of South American nations on peace, development and social justice [The ELN want international involvement in Colombia and the region]
- Government creates a peace congress before asking ELN to enter peace talks
- A national vote for peace calling on the ELN to negotiate

- A camp for the ELN / FARC-EP where social leaders, students, representatives of political organisations, and ordinary people can come to make contact and start debates with guerillas

Social Justice

- A fast-track court for political crimes [killing of politicians]
- Colombian universities working with local grassroots organisations on projects / passing on ideas
- Try violations of armed forces in civilian courts
- Compensation for those who are arrested and detained who are not convicted of any crimes
- Publicise threats to people in the national media and profile them
- Social investments in regions dominated by FARC-EP / ELN
- More investment in reform institutions that already exist
- Municipal level task forces for peace and development work with communities / civil societies – COPY THE WORK OF NGO's here
- FARC-EP / ELN passing on information about drug traffickers / drug leaders if a peace agreement is signed
- A one-time wealth tax to fund demobilization and reintegration of FARC-EP / ELN combatants
- Improve certain medical services country-wide
- Provide legal advice centres across the country
- Government provides a LARGER grant to people in place of regular social assistance payments five to six times a year
- Colombian expatriates in USA and other major countries send "remittances" to Colombian municpality offices. The money is used for development projects. Civil society are involved in these projects. Colombian government matches money on a three to one basis. Look at the example of Mexico. The municipality inform migrants of projects developed.
- Adult education for women combined with vocational training to make them attend – empowering women is the best way to combat poverty
- School feeding programmes for children – parents will be more willing to send their children to school

- Exemptions from all school fees for children in poor municipalities for primary and secondary schooling
- Release FARC-EP / ELN prisoners in stages during negotiations – Church assisting prisoners who are released

Reforms

- A program to deal with displaced people
- A mobile micro-credit bank in rural areas [start on a trial basis] to assist peasants
- Nationalise health care
- A law against monopolization in financial / agricultural / commercial and mining sectors :- break up industries if necessary
- A peace tax
- A "LARGE" government fund to help finance NGO projects

Land

- Government leasing land from landlords to give to peasants :- long-term leases : eventually they own the land
- Taxes on lands that are not occupied and or not cultivated
- Allow community ownership of land
- Take land reform out of the hands of the government :- a commission composed of community / union and environmental representatives. Give it the necessary legal powers and financing.
- Cancel all debts owed by peasants to the government "an amnesty"
- Peasants registering land locally that is abandoned
- If tenants abandon land they can hand ownership of it over to the community
- An end to aerial fumigation in FARC-EP / ELN controlled areas
- Make land registration for small landholders free
- Allow groups of small farmers to take out a loan together
- Designating agricultural land use in certain areas – prevent landholders from appropriating land and using it for cattle ranching [which requires very few workers]
- Simplify the rules on resolving the land conflicts
- Credit to rural community-level groups to assist rural farmers
- Land reform institutes in each state – central bureaucracies are less effective

- Farmers can rent community owned land – money raised is invested locally
- A review of Colombia's land reform institution what works where the flaws are
- Add women's names to land titles alongside their husbands names
- Cash grants to small farmers who buy or rent small farms to develop their farms
- A peasants institute – for policy development / research / empowering peasants

Negotiations

- No extradition of terrorists to the USA
- Release of all FARC-EP / ELN prisoners
- Civil society assembly putting forward issues and recommendations for a peace talks
- FARC-EP and ELN can consult with a civil society committee appointed by civil society assembly during talks
- FARC-EP and ELN attend workshops on conflict resolution provided by a US college that specializes in peace
- Government insisting FARC-EP and ELN acknowledge public opposition to "kidnappings"
- Finance the ELN/FARC-EP to carryout de-mining activities
- Social reform proposals that are not agreed upon can be put before parliament for it to decide upon
- Reach out to FARC-EP and ELN "We recognise that the FARC's agenda, and the ELN's is not revolutionary, socialist, maximalist or intransigent, but is in fact, more or less within the scope of much of the contemporary left in present-day Latin America"
- Government provide food, clothing, other items plus income subsistence per member to the ELN/FARC-EP during ceasefire. In return they pledge not to commit any kidnappings / to release all kidnapped persons and not to purchase any arms
- Talk to FARC-EP / ELN prisoners in prison get their ideas on peace. Their suggestions to their movements
- FARC-EP / ELN can meet informally with other political parties in Colombia
- Government :- make a significant concession at start of negotiations to get positive movement in talks

- Roman Catholic Church intervening at crucial stages where there is disagreement and they make the decision
- After an agreement – both sides in negotiations visit European other developed nations governments explaining a peace agreement to get aid to finance the peace agreement
- Teams to negotiate in each of the major issue areas
- Church contacting ELN for initial talks
- Catholic church attend meetings between government and FARC-EP / ELN as an observer
- Government must talk to members of central command of ELN and not just to its leader

Policing

- Ban the sale of alcohol after 1pm in cities and town centers
- A woman's night out on the town : only women allowed on the city centre streets [no men]
- Get mayors in each city to publish crime statistics. This will prevent hard-line city councillors from rejecting further police reforms and from abandoning current reforms. Publicise data at press conferences / community briefings / newsletters
- Community meetings which are attended by police officials where citizens discuss how the police could be more accountable to city residents. This forces the police to engage in dialogue with varied social sectors that it has long lacked accountability to + forcing hard-line politicians in city councils to accept further reforms
- Community policing begins after extensive training where community police officers spend several days conducting surveys at each residence and business in their assigned neighbourhood. There are two purposes for this : 1. To introduce police officers to community residences and generate public interest. 2. They provide officers with a preliminary assessment of the principal concerns specific to the community – providing info not just on citizen security but other social problems as well.
- Local communities involved in recruiting members to the police force Participatory Budgeting
- Public meetings with city officials – make people aware of the issues

- Empower citizens to vote on where development resources are allocated [citizens must make decisions within budget constraints]. Citizens vote on projects
- Officials develop "Quality of life" indexes to make citizens aware of where social justice resources need to be allocated
- Make citizens aware of where spending is going
- Participatory Budgeting generally leads to social justice-inspired change
- Citizens attending meetings regularly will start organising together

DEMOCRACY

ERITREA

Issues :

- Dictatorship
- Political Prisoners
- National One-party system
- Regional Political Parties

Those Involved

- Eritrean Government
- AU
- Ethiopia

Those Working For Peace :

- United Nations In Ethiopia And Eritrea [UNMEE]
- Organisation Of Eritrean Americans

SYRIA

Issues :

- Civil War
- Dominant Single Party / restrictive democracy
- Effective Dictator

People Involved :

- Arab Neighbours - Iran / Turkey / Saudi Arabia
- Free Syrian Army [Rebel Movement]
- Syrian Government

Those Working For Peace :

- Arab League
- International Community
- UN Envoy Lakhdar Brahimi
- Unity Community Organisation And Enlightment Trust

DEMOCRACY IDEAS

- First Step - allow access by human rights groups to political prisoners
- NGO's meeting with government to produce - policy documents
- Highlight government decisions to foreign countries
- International media questioning president
- Broadcast parliamentary meetings on television and on radio
- Permit Lobby Groups - from various categories e.g. women's organisations; business federation; religious leaders - This is before a multi-party democracy
- Police are not allowed to carry weapons on them
- No mass demonstrations by government - The president should keep his ego in check
- An arbitrator independently appointed by president to negotiate with opposition
- Get independent organisations from outside the country to do surveys of the people - what they think of their leader; other issues - They fill out a form and post it to the external organisation
- Government ministers be brave enough to voice opposition to decisions
- Opposition parties can publish their manifestos in the media
- Invitations by western governments to leaders of these autocratic regimes
- Politicians and the president must retire at a certain age
- Retire from the military and join politics as a civilian - This is what the current president of Myanmar did.
- Allow for trade unions for each employment sector
- Can only be president for a certain number of terms
- NGO's / Trade Union leaders allowed to enter politics
- Call for your successor to be a civilian
- Put members of opposition parties into your government
- Develop meeting places - where Eritreans can regularly discuss politics, voice complaints, petition for redress - Choose politicians to go to these meetings
- Can criticise officials but not the president

- Allow for the establishment of private law agencies
- Allow media to be present at court hearings to ensure fair hearings
- Freedom of press to comment on external news
- International NGOs have to appoint local people to lead in the country
- Can resign from the military and enter politics - This was done in Myanmar
- Debates on television with politicians
- Can form new political parties while elected
- A youth parliament which can pass motions and submit them to the actual parliament
- An outside force training politicians in democratic principles - how to negotiate / collaborate with each other
- Can have different political parties running regional / provincial governments
- Reassure these leaders that the transition to democracy will be peaceful - Give examples of Chile, Turkey, Korea and Thailand
- Trade union movements can have their own political parties
- Appoint someone as your successor if you wish to leave politics
- Have to have a certain level of education to participate in elections
- Have a league of women voters organisation
- Ask foreign nations to cancel your debts in return for democracy reform
- To the EU print money and give it to reforming countries
- Set bonus political seats for large parties in parliament - prevent too many small parties from forming and competing - smaller parties will probably coalesce together.
- Set up an interim government. This should include as many political parties as possible.
- The president appoints the prime minister who chooses a cabinet
- Important leaders visiting the leader or inviting them to visit you
- Leader of country - stays on as president in a largely ceremonial role for a seven year period
- UNESCO drawing up educational texbooks for schools
- Release of political prisoners

- Give the business community a special role in government - Minister for industry and
- employment chosen by them
- Resolve territorial disputes
- Establish credit unions across the country to deal with poverty
- Religious leaders visiting President Afewerki and affirming in public he is committed
- to democracy
- Military cannot enter politics - However they can resign from the army and then enter politics
- The eldest son inherits the land - avoid constantly dividing up the land
- Schools should be secular with a special day set aside for religious teaching in church or mosque settings
- Religious organisations being involved in charity - Declared as NGO's with no taxes on them
- Negotiators of new constitution [from all political parties and from a civil society assembly] going before parliament and explaining their decisions
- Human rights developed by people of notable backgrounds - including the president's wife who would lead such a committee
- An international peace institute for Eritrea - funded by the AU and lead by the president
- Education - teaching pupils what has been is being done on peace in other countries

PRESIDENTS POWERS

1. The president can hold office for seven years - one term of office
2. President can appoint senior judiciary
3. If parliament cannot agree by majority on an issue - Then the president decides
4. The president can dissolve parliament on the request of the cabinet and new elections within 40 days. A judicial body would administer government for the 40 days
5. President governs an international peace institute
6. I would ask the AU to request Eritrea be given a seat on the UN security council in recognition for President Afewerki's progress towards democracy

- Politicians cannot own media outlets

- A council of journalists to deal with censorship and rate media agencies for their factual and interesting reporting
- Youth journalists attached to major media outlets
- A printing press that more than one media outlet can use - saving them production
- Costs
- Governments should have a right to reply in media outlets
- EGO deflator - Say it as it is in the country. The president is fallible
- Elections : Equal free air-time for all parties | Politicians stationing their own representatives at polling booths to prevent vote rigging | Vote for parties not individuals. The percentage each party gets determines the number of seats they can have
- A branch within the police specifically to investigate corruption
- A minister for corruption
- Get individual politicians across the political divide [different parties] to join together on combating corruption
- Business surveys to highlight levels of corruption
- Business can fill out government forms over the internet to avoid levels of corruption
- Politicians have to declare all their income sources [including you Mr. President]
- Media publicising corruption
- A judicial body to investigate corruption
- Rewards for reporting corruption if it shows to be true
- Judges are in charge of appointing senior civil service members
- A business integrity forum - to ensure businesses do not have to give bribes to people.
- Limit the amount of money businesses can give to political parties - all business may only donate to parties and not to individuals
- Employ foreigners alongside judiciary to investigate corruption
- Politicians can register to have their finances investigated by the judiciary - Establish their credentials as "clean" politicians

- Politicians including the president cannot have shares or ownership over state assets
- Establish a citizen report card - to survey citizens opinions / experiences of various state companies / state ministries. The results would be publicised in the media
- Establish credit unions - Money for social welfare payments is made direct from government accounts to credit unions - eliminating corruption at the various levels
- A social welfare payment 4 - 5 times a year instead of regular social welfare payments
- Children write letters to President Afewerki - the winning essay from each school is passed on to the president
- The president cannot be a leader of a political party [can be a member of it though]
- Politicians must have certain level of education and be literate to compete in elections - This was done in Pakistan by former president Pervez Musharraf.
- "Mandate parties" campaigning around an issue - Islam / political reform / employment / corruption etc.
- Set up a democracy institute for Eritrea and the rest of the world
- Embassy officials of different governments can question government ministers - call them to meet with them
- Freedom of speech - politicians from the ruling party attending these speeches and assuring those speaking of their safety
- Reduce Military budget - Keep military busy in UN peacekeeping missions | cooperation in international training for military
- An apology for wrongdoings - would be reciprocated
- A branch within the police specifically to investigate corruption
- A minister for corruption
- Get individual politicians across the political divide [different parties] to join together on combating corruption
- Business surveys to highlight levels of corruption

- Business can fill out government forms over the internet to avoid levels of corruption
- Politicians have to declare all their income sources [including you Mr. President]
- Media publicising corruption
- Rewards for reporting corruption if it shows to be true
- Judges are in charge of appointing senior civil service members
- A business integrity forum - to ensure businesses do not have to give bribes to people.
- Limit the amount of money businesses can give to political parties - all business may only donate to parties and not to individuals
- Politicians can register to have their finances investigated by the judiciary - Establish their credentials as "clean" politicians
- Politicians including the president cannot have shares or ownership over state assets
- Establish a citizen report card - to survey citizens opinions / experiences of various state companies / state ministries. The results would be publicised in the media
- A UN workshop on corruption for politicians in a country
- A minister for corruption - drawn from civil society
- An international court in the country appointed by the AU to deal with corruption; validating elections - Reasons for this local judiciary is not skilled enough - concerns that local judiciary may not be as efficient due to lack of funding
- International police training for investigations / audits of people's finances
- Community groups - individuals joining together when seeking financing / applications for services - may reduce corruption
- NGO's can talk direct to the president about corruption
- Appointing judiciary with approval of parliament
- Party financing must be made public - who supported them
- Political parties must have a party support base of people | must garner at least 1,000 signatures to form a party
- Political leaders must have their finances investigated
- Party base nominates those who can become politicians after any elections

- Protect those in the civil service who expose corruption
- Media presence at court cases | especially corruption cases
- Media can have access to public service to audit where money is being "lost" along the chain of bureaucracy
- Must vote for a party rather than individual politicians - reduces corruption such as
- buying votes / politicians doing favours for people
- Reform within the police by the police
- Making people aware of the consequences of corruption. They will be less likely to give in to corruption or   accept it
- Force new legislation on corruption by gathering votes from across the political divide
- in parliament
- To eliminate corruption at various levels - pay social welfare payments direct to local credit unions / post offices
- Instead of regular social welfare payments which the government cannot afford - have larger payments paid 4 -5 times a year
- President cannot be leader of a party [can be a member of one though]
- Mandate parties campaigning around a single issue - Islamic / Christian / political reform / Employment / corruption
- Set up a democracy institute
- An ex-presidential fund to do good works
- Allow NGO's to speak at Universities / allow debates in college among students / commemorating those who have died who did good works - Politicians assure them of their safety to speak
- Keep military busy : involve them in UN peacekeeping missions - other countries fund the military costs of this / Joint military training with a country in the west
- Media Rights : Right of response for government to media articles
- Parliamentary cross-party committees on investigations into journalists being persecuted / killed

- In libel laws burden of proof must lie with the complainant rather than the journalist
- A human rights commission to regulate journalism
- Negotiators should go before parliament and explain their decisions
  - Parliamentary oversight bodies
  - Citizens tracking budgetary expenditures

PURPOSE OF MEDIA

- To hold officials to account by acting as a "watchdog" that brings misuses of power or policy failures to the knowledge of the public
  - To provide citizens with the information they need to participate in society
  - To serve as a forum for different views both official and alternative - to mobilise support for a cause
  - The media must be a moral agency
  - The role of the media is to expand knowledge and overcome biases
- Newspapers can publish contradictory articles journalists on each side taking a side
- on an issue
  - In elections newspapers television must publish the goals of all political parties as they are written
  - A "nationwide" programme to highlight good works being done all around the country
- A Reuters style news agency for Eritrea - government financed - run by national journalists union - insist on factual / accurate news reporting from the agency
- There must be a separation between media ownership and editorial decision-making

ERITREA

Purpose : To change Eritrea into a democracy

Strategy : Give respect to their leader [give respect get respect].Stage the ideas over a few years. Encourage him and reassure his future role as ceremonial president. That he is safe from facing persecution.

KEYWORDS

"Human Rights Groups" "Political Prisoners" "Parliamentary Meetings" "Military Spending" "Lobby Groups" "International NGO's" "Youth Parliament" "Interim Government" "UNESCO" "President Isaias Afewerki" "Credit Unions" "Poverty" "Religion" "Human Rights" "Peace Institute" "Media Rights" "Corruption" "Elections" "Police Corruption" "Mandate Parties" "Military Budget"

- FIRST STEP - ALLOW ACCESS BY HUMAN RIGHTS GROUPS TO POLITICAL PRISONERS

#1 TO ERITREAN PRESIDENT ISAIAS AFEWERKI - ALLOW ACCESS BY HUMAN RIGHTS GROUPS TO POLITICAL PRISONERS

21/05/2015 - 4/05/2015

TO ERITREAN PRESIDENT

Dear Ambassador,

Please can you pass the following on to President Afewerki.

Dear Mr. President

I want bring democracy to your country and I need your help to do this. I don't support mass protests or demonstrations. I don't support revolutions AND I promise you I will not work for this. A lot of countries have political prisoners - If I had my way I would change that everywhere. I'm starting with you - Amnesty International are a credible human rights group - they state that there have been over 10,000 political prisoners over the last 20 years in your country. Prisons do not reform people - for political prisoners they only attract attention - the wrong kind. The first step on the road to democracy is to allow international human rights groups access to these prisoners AND let families of the detained know their whereabouts and visit them. Show compassion here to the families - the families do not have to meet with these human rights groups. These prisoners upon release could promise not to condemn the government but to work only for democracy - by working with your government - helping your country make friends in the world [you don't have enough friends] Telling them things are going to change. They could form political NGO'S to produce policy documents for your government. If you tell me you will work for

125

democracy I will believe you.. This change is going to take several years [I reckon 3 years as an optimum] This is the first step on the road to democracy. Thank You For Taking The Time To Read This Letter Mr. President. - I will write to you again.

- SECOND STEP - ALLOW BROADCASTS OVER THE RADIO AND TELEVISION OF PARLIAMENTARY MEETINGS

#2 TO ERITREAN PRESIDENT ISAIAS AFEWERKI - ALLOW BROADCASTS OVER THE RADIO AND TELEVISION OF PARLIAMENTARY MEETINGS

11/06/2015 - 18/06/2015
TO ERITREAN PRESIDENT
Dear Ambassador,
Please can you pass the following on to President Afewerki.
Dear Mr. President
The next step to democracy is this : Broadcast parliamentary meetings on television and / or radio. It will force politicians to be more open and people will believe in their politicians - that decisions are being made by them. The appearance from abroad is that only the president and his own political party have power - Prove them wrong. This means putting journalists in parliament. Do you think you can do this? Thank You For Taking The Time To Read This Letter Mr. President. - I will write to you again.

- THIRD STEP - END MASS DEMONSTRATIONS FOR THE LEADER AND REDUCE MILITARY SPENDING

#3 TO ERITREAN PRESIDENT ISAIAS AFEWERKI - END MASS DEMONSTRATIONS FOR THE LEADER AND REDUCE MILITARY SPENDING

25/06/2015
TO ERITREAN PRESIDENT
Dear Ambassador,
Please can you pass the following on to President Afewerki.
Dear Mr. President
This is a common problem with single leaders - All power rests with you. Ego is something you are always combating if you are someone important or successful. Your ego should only be as

high as you are [same for others]. Displays of power such as mass demonstrations - I have to clarify as negative for your ego. You are someone important with a lot of responsibility. But the message has to be clear - no mass demonstrations or your ego will go unchecked. Most countries don't have mass demonstrations. In my country there are no mass demonstrations by government. You would be a good leader if you followed this policy of constantly keeping your ego in check. Mass demonstrations do not make you more popular. I'll give you a secret, sometime to come, wars and militarism will end all over the world. Mass demonstrations give a negative image abroad. Look after your people and spend less on the military - the latter a difficult decision I know. Thank you Mr President for taking the time to read this email - I will write to you again.

- FOURTH STEP - ALLOW INDEPENDENT FOREIGN AGENCIES TO DO SURVEYS OF THE PEOPLE

#4 TO ERITREAN PRESIDENT ISAIAS AFEWERKI ALLOW INDEPENDENT FOREIGN AGENCIES TO DO SURVEYS OF THE PEOPLE

2/07/2015

TO ERITREAN PRESIDENT

Dear Ambassador,

Please can you pass the following on to President Afwerki.

Dear Mr. President

This next step is a big one; Get independent organisations from outside the country to do surveys of the people - what they think of their leader; other issues - They fill out a form and post it to the external organisation. This will give people the confidence to express themselves. I don't think you want total control over your people. I don't think you intend being afraid of your own people. I don't think the people will rebel against you. Don't be afraid of what happens. Your image abroad will certainly improve. I know the risk - people may wish they had a different leader. Are you prepared to go through with this - It does mean change. There is a saying "a week in politics is a long time". You are not going to lose your job over this. Thank you Mr President for taking the time to read this email - I will write to you again

- FIFTH STEP - ALLOW LOBBY GROUPS TO WORK IN YOUR COUNTRY

#5 TO ERITREAN PRESIDENT ISAIAS AFEWERKI- ALLOW LOBBY GROUPS TO WORK IN YOUR COUNTRY

9/07/2015 - 23/07/2015

TO ERITREAN PRESIDENT

Dear Ambassador,

Please can you pass the following on to President Afewerki.

Dear Mr. President

Before democracy comes and I think you are committed to this. Allow lobby groups - Use the people who are already there on the ground for this [such as NGOs, regional political parties] - they can meet the president, and please let them talk to other politicians as well. Please and thank you. There is a lot of work here to be done. Okay you are still in charge - but I hope you accept my suggestions. Thank you Mr President for taking the time to read this email - I will write to you again.

- SIXTH STEP - INTERNATIONAL NGOS

#6 TO ERITREAN PRESIDENT ISAIAS AFEWERKI - INTERNATIONAL NGOS

27/08/2015

TO ERITREAN PRESIDENT

Dear Ambassador,

Please can you pass the following on to President Afewerki.

Dear Mr. President

I know you are a cautious country - But this is another step on the road to democracy : Allow in International NGOs to pair with local NGO's. Most NGO's do not want to trouble the government - although there must be space for a call to changes. As long as they are not protesting on the streets - I think you should allow them. Thank you Mr President for taking the time to read this email - I will write to you again.

- SEVENTH STEP - PUT MEMBERS OF OPPOSITION PARTIES INTO YOUR GOVERNMENT

#7 TO ERITREAN PRESIDENT ISAIAS AFEWERKI - PUT MEMBERS OF OPPOSITION PARTIES INTO YOUR GOVERNMENT

3/09/2015 - 17/09/2015

TO ERITREAN PRESIDENT

Dear Ambassador,

Please can you pass the following on to President Afewerki.

Dear Mr. President

Put members of opposition parties into your government. You would have more credibility abroad - this is another step on the road to democracy. It doesn't cost you anything - Your popularity in the country would probably rise considerably. Many sanctions against your country could be lifted if you take this step. This policy has been tried in other countries such as Thailand on the road to democracy. Thank you Mr President for taking the time to read this email - I will write to you again.

- EIGHT STEP - DEVELOP MEETING PLACES - WHERE ERITREANS CAN REGULARLY DISCUSS POLITICS, VOICE COMPLAINTS - YOUR GOVERNMENT SHOULD CHOOSE POLITICIANS TO ATTEND THESE MEETINGS

#8 TO ERITREAN PRESIDENT ISAIAS AFEWERKI - DEVELOP MEETING PLACES - WHERE ERITREANS CAN DISCUSS ISSUES WITH POLITICIANS

24/09/2015

TO ERITREAN PRESIDENT

Dear Ambassador,

Please can you pass the following on to President Afewerki.

Dear Mr. President

Develop meeting places - where Eritreans can regularly discuss politics, voice complaints, petition for redress - Your government should choose politicians to go to these meetings. We are talking about openness here - make people feel they are being listened to and politicians will have more work to do - there will be better legislation. It will make people feel that change is coming. Thank you Mr President for taking the time to read this email - I will write to you again.

- NINTH STEP - AN EMOTIONAL LETTER

#9 TO ERITREAN PRESIDENT ISAIAS AFEWERKI - AN EMOTIONAL LETTER

1/10/2015

TO ERITREAN PRESIDENT

Dear Ambassador,

Please can you pass the following on to President Afewerki

Dear Mr President

I am sorry that the world has isolated you. I do think you are a capable leader. I do believe you care deeply about your country. I would criticise that you are not a democracy - but I believe all you need is help to achieve that. I just want you to know I consider you a friend and want to help you transform your country. This journey is going to require commitment and courage; you will have problems; there will be days when you are discouraged; you may have enemies who do not want change. But there will be a happy ending. I do not criticise your sins - I am a sinner myself - everyone is. What matters is what you do now. Do not be afraid - be brave

- TENTH STEP - SET UP A YOUTH PARLIAMENT

#10 TO ERITREAN PRESIDENT ISAIAS AFEWERKI - SET UP A YOUTH PARLIAMEN

29/10/2015 - 19/11/2015

TO ERITREAN PRESIDENT

Dear Ambassador,

Please can you pass the following on to President Afewerki

Dear Mr President,

I propose a youth parliament. I will make no hidden meanings here. Young people are more open-minded and want change more than adults. There real power would be moral force - by submitting their proposals to the proper parliament their proposals would have to be debated. Here are young people influencing your country. This parliament should meet regularly at least once a month. I know this is pressure to reform - so be it.

- ELEVENTH STEP - BONUS SEATS FOR LARGE PARTIES

#11 TO ERITREAN PRESIDENT ISAIAS AFEWERKI - BONUS SEATS FOR LARGE PARTIES

26/11/2015 - 31/12/2015

TO ERITREAN PRESIDENT

Dear Ambassador,

Please can you pass the following on to President Afewerki

Dear Mr President

A common problem with new democracies is that there are too many fragmented parties. You have to try and please everyone to get anything done which does not work. I propose that you give bonus seats to large parties. This will force small parties to coalesce together to maintain influence.

- TWELFTH STEP - INTERIM GOVERNMENT - PRESIDENCY CHANGED TO A CEREMONIAL ROLE

#12 TO ERITREAN PRESIDENT ISAIAS AFEWERKI - INTERIM GOVERNMENT - PRESIDENCY CHANGED TO A CEREMONIAL ROLE

7/01/2016

TO ERITREAN PRESIDENT

Dear Ambassador,

Please can you pass the following on to President Afewerki

Dear Mr President

Stay committed to democracy. Stay committed to democracy. This is the road that you are directing. There can be no half measures or else it is not democracy. Democracy is not perfect but it is the best system out there. When the times comes. I would support you staying on as president [in a ceremonial role - you will have some poltical rights] for an seven year period once democracy is fully introduced. It is going to take courage and perseverance to see this through. We have a president in Ireland - I would ask you to investigate what roles the president here fulfils and copy it. Before you finish in government you must set up an interim government to lead the way to democratic elections - this should be comprised of as many political parties in your country as possible. This is your last task before democracy. Will you do this - will you go all the way?

- THIRTEENTH STEP - POWERS OF THE PRESIDENT

#13 TO ERITREAN PRESIDENT ISAIAS AFEWERKI - POWERS OF THE PRESIDENT

14/01/2016 - 28/01/2016

TO ERITREAN PRESIDENT

Dear Ambassador,

Please can you pass the following on to President Afewerki

Dear Mr President

I would establish your rights as president :

1. The president can hold office for seven years - one term of office

2. President can appoint senior judiciary

3. If parliament cannot agree by majority on an issue - Then the president decides

4. The president can dissolve parliament on the request of the cabinet and new elections within 40 days. A judicial body would administer government for the 40 days

5. President governs an international peace institute

6. I would ask the AU to request Eritrea be given a seat on the UN security council in recognition for President Afewerki's progress towards democracy

RELIGIOUS SUPPORTING PRESIDENT AFEWERKI

FOR HIS EXCELLENCY ABUNE MENGHISTEAB TESFAMARIAM - RELIGIOUS SUPPORTING PRESIDENT AFEWERKI

4/02/2016 - 11/02/2016

Your Excellency Abune Menghisteab Tesfamariam,

I am asking for your help. I want to bring democracy to Eritrea - indeed the president may have already started on this course. I need you to cooperate with the other Christian churches and Muslim leaders in Eritrea on this. I need you both to visit president Afewerki and assure him of your support for the work he is doing to bring democracy. I want you to assure him that he is not threatened in anyway in the future. I have proposed to President Afewerki that he remain on as president in a largely ceremonial role for a seven year period - he would have some political rights. I want you all to state publicly to the media that you believe that the president is committed to democracy and that you support him. I am trusting you with a secret - You may check out all the emails I have sent to President Afewerki and all the emails I will be sending to him at http://www.peace-implementation.info/eritrea_democracy_proposal.html Eritrea Democracy Proposal. Please do not disclose this link to anyone.

• FOURTEENTH STEP - UNESCO DRAWING UP EDUCATIONAL TEXTBOOKS

#14 TO ERITREAN PRESIDENT ISAIAS AFEWERKI - UNESCO DRAWING UP EDUCATIONAL TEXTBOOKS

11/02/2016 - 11/03/2016

TO ERITREAN PRESIDENT

Dear Ambassador,

Please can you pass the following on to President Afewerki

Dear Mr President

I recommend that you ask UNESCO to draw up educational textbooks for your schools. UNESCO are pretty good at their job. The material can be appropriate to the religion in your country and respectful of your president. If you want to develop your country education is the first step. I would take a slice out of the military budget and use it for universal education up to the age of 16. I want your country to be prosperous and I provide you with a link http://www.peace-implementation.info/employment_ideas.html that provides ideas for creating employment but first you must educate your students. Ask neighbouring countries to set up university campuses in your country - a quick way to develop third level education.

- FIFTEENTH STEP - RELEASE OF POLITICAL PRISONERS

#15 TO ERITREAN PRESIDENT ISAIAS AFEWERKI - RELEASE OF POLITICAL PRISONERS

18/03/2016

TO ERITREAN PRESIDENT

Dear Ambassador,

Please can you pass the following on to President Afewerki

Dear Mr President

The next step is releasing political prisoners. Why do you do this when they spoke against you. You do it for two reasons 1. It is a tradition within Islam to release prisoners during Ramadan and 2. You are saying I can be criticised [I am not desperate to hold on to power which you are not]. I think they are going to change their minds about you when they see what you are doing.

- SIXTEENTH STEP - ALLOWING BUSINESS COMMUNITY TO CHOOSE MINISTER FOR INDUSTRY AND EMPLOYMENT

#16 TO ERITREAN PRESIDENT ISAIAS AFEWERKI - ALLOWING BUSINESS COMMUNITY TO CHOOSE MINISTER FOR INDUSTRY AND EMPLOYMENT

15/03/2106 - 22/03/2016

TO ERITREAN PRESIDENT

Dear Ambassador,

Please can you pass the following on to President Afewerki

Dear Mr President

Try something new here - that the democratic west has not seen. Allow the minister of industry and employment to be chosen by the business community. One of their members. They have the experience necessary to do their job well. Other countries may copy you.

- SEVENTEENTH STEP - RESOLVING TERRITORIAL DISPUTES

#17 TO ERITREAN PRESIDENT ISAIAS AFEWERKI - RESOLVING TERRITORIAL DISPUTES

19/04/2016

TO ERITREAN PRESIDENT

Dear Ambassador,

Please can you pass the following on to President Afewerki

Dear Mr President

With regard to your territorial disputes with Ethiopia - I would invite the AU to once again send a commission to determine the boundaries between your two nations. Ethiopia would be under significant psychological pressure to accept their findings - rather than default twice after having said it would accept the commission's findings for a second time. In your dispute with Yemen over the Hanish islands - a possible agreement would be one country to own the islands and the other country control the fishing rights around the islands. With regard to your territorial dispute with Djibouti - I would withdraw to the boundaries that had existed. Once the boundary dispute is solved it would be interesting to see you visit the President of Ethiopia - go to his country - his home. Be seen shaking hands with him change from being enemies to being friends. You don't have a lot of friends at the moment in the countries surrounding you - I am sorry for that - Ethiopia is a big step towards changing that. There is a precedent here Anwar Sadat former president of Egypt went to Israel to meet with their prime minister - He spoke about peace before the Knesset. You can do the same with Ethiopia.

- EIGHTEENTH STEP - A SECOND EMOTIONAL LETTER

#18 TO ERITREAN PRESIDENT ISAIAS AFeWERKI - A SECOND EMOTIONAL LETTER

26/04/2016

TO ERITREAN PRESIDENT

Dear Ambassador,

Please can you pass the following on to your President

Dear Mr. President

Your people are going to love you for bringing democracy. You will have a place in history. To achieve being president you must be a very capable leader. One of the pillars of democracy is elections including for the presidency. If you want this system to work and I believe you do you are going to have to see this right through to the end. There can be no half measures no permanent president [what do you think of this] If you were in political opposition what would you do for the state ? Listen to the calls for democracy - they do exist. The best thing you can do is hand over to a stable government. Research has shown that where a country holds two successive elections - they are more likely to survive as a democracy. Since you will be president for eight years you will probably see your country through these elections [hopefully] successfully.

- NINETEENTH STEP - ALLOW FOR THE ESTABLISHMENT OF PRIVATE LAW AGENCIES

#19 TO ERITREAN PRESIDENT ISAIAS AFEWERKI - ALLOW FOR THE ESTABLISHMENT OF PRIVATE LAW AGENCIES

3/05/2016 - 10/05/2016
TO ERITREAN PRESIDENT
Dear Ambassador,
Please can you pass the following on to President Afewerki
Dear Mr. President,
Allow for the establishment of private law agencies. Law agencies represent people. A real democracy empowers people. Actively pariticpate in society. You can say it is 50/50 that people will benefit from this issue. Governments are supposed to accept criticism and change. I stress supposed to... If people can challenge the government - they will believe in you as a just and fair country. It is not going to cost you your job. I think any system in the world claims to represent the people whether it is North Korea or Ireland. NGO's would be most likely to be empowered by this. To quote a noble laureate it is NGO's that will save the world in the future. Everything I do is about this - saving the world. I hope my ideas work with you if they do then they are reusable for other countries with conservative governments. I am guessing that Eritreans are good people. So the key point to make here is that you should allow law agencies establish themselves in your country. You could be like former Russian president Mikhail Gorbachev who introduced "Glasnost and Perestroika" - "truth and openness". Law agencies ensure this kind of work. Also media should be allowed to be present at court hearings to ensure fair hearings.

- TWENTIETH STEP - CREDIT UNIONS AND POVERTY

#20 TO ERITREAN PRESIDENT ISAIAS AFEWERKI - CREDIT UNIONS AND POVERTY

7/06/2016 - 12/07/2016

TO ERITREAN PRESIDENT

Dear Ambassador,

Please can you pass the following on to President Afewerki

Dear Mr President

The best way out of poverty is credit unions. Unfortunately a common problem with third world countries is corruption. I propose that the government funds in banks directly transfer money to local credit unions for village councils to use thus eliminating corruption at the different levels. Since it would cost too much to provide regular social welfare - I propose that the government via such credit unions would make a larger payment 4 - 5 a year to families. Also with education - parents could be paid a small stipend every three month [a weeks wages] for sending their children to school [all the way to completing secondary school]. This also they would receive via the credit union. Also the children can receive free school lunches.

- TWENTY-FIRST STEP - A FEW SUGGESTIONS

#21 TO ERITREAN PRESIDENT ISAIAS AFEWERKI - A FEW SUGGESTIONS

19/07/2016

TO ERITREAN PRESIDENT

Dear Ambassador,

Please can you pass the following on to President Afewerki

Dear Mr President

A few suggestions - I would prevent the military from entering politics - However a military person can resign from the army and then enter politics. This is what happened in Myanmar with general Than Shwe who became president of Myanmar in the past. Allow politicians to hold press conferences. Create a human rights court - it does not have to be big and also a Human Rights Ombudsman with regard to issues of state. With regard to inheritance of land - I would choose the eldest son to inherit all the land rather than continually shrinking the land by constantly dividing it up.

- TWENTY-SECOND STEP - RELIGION

#22 TO ERITREAN PRESIDENT ISAIAS AFEWERKI - RELIGION

30/08/2016 - 6/09/2016

TO ERITREAN PRESIDENT

Dear Ambassador,

Please can you pass the following on to President Afewerki

Dear Mr President

I have two points to make with regard for religion. The first is that education should be secular but that there should be a special day chosen for religious education in church or mosque settings. The second point I want to make is that religious organisations both Christian and Muslim should be involved in charity work and should be classified as NGO's with no taxes on them

- TWENTY-THIRD STEP - HUMAN RIGHTS

#23 TO ERITREAN PRESIDENT ISAIAS AFEWERKI- HUMAN RIGHTS

11/11/2016 - 25/11/2016

TO ERITREAN PRESIDENT

Dear Ambassador,

Please can you pass the following on to President Afewerki

Dear Mr President

Human rights legislation developed by a committee - including women's rights - involve men and women of notable backgrounds including the president's wife who leads this committee.

International training for police - Involve as many agencies as you can on this - AU / EU / UN.

Have international representation on Human Rights / Press freedoms Ombudsman board.

- TWENTY-FOURTH STEP - PEACE INSTITUTE

#24 TO ERITREAN PRESIDENT ISAIAS AFEWERKI - PEACE INSTITUTE

23/12/2016

TO ERITREAN PRESIDENT

Dear Ambassador,

Please can you pass the following on to President Afewerki

Dear Mr President

Develop an international peace institute for Eritrea - the AU would fund this and the president would lead such a body. Education - teach peace - what is being done in other countries on peace in Africa and the rest of the world.

- TWENTY-FIFTH STEP - MEDIA RIGHTS

#25 TO ERITREAN PRESIDENT ISAIAS AFEWERKI - MEDIA RIGHTS

30/12/2016 - 27/02/2017

TO ERITREAN PRESIDENT

Dear Ambassador,

Please can you pass the following on to President Afewerki

Dear Mr President

Can have state publications along with other media outlets. There should be free access to the internet. Politicians cannot own media outlets [If they did - journalists could end up being biased in their reporting]. Implement international laws on freedom of press - Get an expert policy group from abroad to work on this. There should be a council of journalists to decide what should be censored - respect for religion; no hate speech; factual reporting. This council should rate media outlets that operate for the public based on factual and interesting reporting. Youth journalists attached to major newspapers. Set up internet centres across the country. A printing press - that more than one media outlet can use for printing purposes - saving them costs of production. Governments should have a right to reply in media outlets.

- TWENTY-SIXTH STEP - A THIRD EMOTIONAL LETTER

#26 TO ERITREAN PRESIDENT ISAIAS AFWERKI - A THIRD EMOTIONAL LETTER

6/03/2017

TO ERITREAN PRESIDENT

Dear Ambassador,

Please can you pass the following on to your President

Dear Mr. President

I want you to know that you deserve the credit for bringing democracy to Eritrea and it will be recorded as such in history. There is a lot of work to be done and I think you are committed to what needs to be done. I think you are a brave man because there are some dangers in pursuing democracy - some interests may not favour it. This is your legacy. Talk to your wife about what you are doing - some women have great wisdom and she could advise you.

Allah Bless You

God Bless You

- TWENTY-SEVENTH STEP - EGO DEFLATOR - CORRUPTION

#27 TO ERITREAN PRESIDENT ISAIAS AFEWERKI - EGO DEFLATOR - CORRUPTION

13/03/2017 - 20/03/2017

TO ERITREAN PRESIDENT

Dear Ambassador,

Please can you pass the following on to President Afewerki

Dear Mr President

A real democracy allows criticism of the government including its president. In my country it is this way - it does not cause a government to fall or its president either. As long as you do not have a big ego and realise that my real contribution is a stable, government which includes the handover of power. You do not face persecution by allowing free media or free political parties. You may not always be in power - you may be rejected at elections are you prepared for this. The top can be a very lonely place if you try to control everything. Is it the fear of loosing your job; of not being in control of protecting your ego - face these fears. A true politician accepts that his job is not permanent or guaranteed. Realise that even if you Mr. President are in opposition - democracy guarantees that you will have certain rights People are afraid in your country and this is a criticism I will make - I think you accept it too. People are afraid to ask questions - they say yes to you and only say what you allow them to say. Now that you realise this - what can you do ? You would be ten times happier if people were genuine with you. You are giving up power but you are gaining happiness. There is a little break between changing from too high an ego; and, then allowing people to be genuine with you. Which do you want ? I know I am criticising you a lot - sometimes we all need ego deflators including myself that we were not as great as we thought we were. You can still be a good man. I don't think you are going to be angry at me for this and in my country I could say this without being arrested ! Mr president can you say you have made a mistake and accept my criticism - that you will try harder for democracy.

- TWENTY-EIGHT - ELECTIONS

#28 TO ERITREAN PRESIDENT ISAIAS AFEWERKI - ELECTIONS

27/03/2017 - 30/03/2017

TO ERITREAN PRESIDENT

Dear Ambassador,

Please can you pass the following on to President Afewerki

Dear Mr President

I hope you can accept the following suggestions. There is nothing new in these ideas - they have already been developed in other countries systems. So I hope you will accept them. Free air-time for all political parties - equal amount of time for all of them. Put forward their manifestos. NGO's can run in elections as a political party. Civil society organisations should visit the president to ask him to ensure that elections for parliament or president are free and fair. Make public statements after elections freely with the permission of the president on whether the elections were free and fair. No campaigning allowed in the final days leading up to elections [3 days]. Politicians can station their own representatives at polling booths to prevent rigging of the vote. The percentage each party gains in elections as a whole decides how many seats they have. Here people are voting for parties and not individuals. The party then decides which people they want represented in the parliament. Something similar has been done in Germany. Mr president do you think my ideas are good enough. In reality you have the tough part - implementing these ideas.

- TWENTY-NINTH - CORRUPTION

#29 TO ERITREAN PRESIDENT ISAIAS AFEWERKI - CORRUPTION

2/04/2017
TO ERITREAN PRESIDENT
Dear Ambassador,
Please can you pass the following on to President Afewerki
Dear Mr President
I'll be honest - my personal opinion is that you have been involved in corruption to one degree or another. You have a decent standard of living compared to the rest of your people. I also suspect that you are providing money to your party politicians to keep them loyal. This is heavy criticism I know but what if it is true. I would put an amnesty [confidential] for past corruption - provided politicians end corrupt activities. It is a sin to be involved in corruption. Can you accept that it is a sin. I am sorry for saying these things and I don't want to threaten your position as president. Corrupt regimes keep people in poverty with just an elite class being wealthy. There will be change - I believe you if you say you will tackle corruption. The west is going to have to help countries like you improve the living standards of everyone. You have sinned - maybe you don't like hearing this but I think it is true. There has to be change - eliminate corruption in politics and businesses please. This was a difficult letter to write but I had to do it.

- THIRTIETH STEP - DEALING WITH CORRUPTION

#30 TO ERITREAN PRESIDENT ISAIAS AFEWERKI - DEALING WITH CORRUPTION

5/04/2017 - 26/04/2017
TO ERITREAN PRESIDENT

Dear Ambassador,

Please can you pass the following on to President Afewerki

Dear Mr President

I have a number of suggestions for tackling corruption. I hope you approve of them. Corruption is endemic in third world countries. Businesses are scared of investing in countries because of corruption. Many companies operate on the black market because it costs too much in bribes to register their company and deal with state agencies. A significant proportion of GDP is taken up with corruption - money that could be used for other things such as education / police / civil service.

CORRUPTION

- A branch within the police specifically to investigate corruption
- A minister for corruption
- Get individual politicians across the political divide [different parties] to join together on combating corruption
- Business surveys to highlight levels of corruption
- Business can fill out government forms over the internet to avoid levels of corruption
- Politicians have to declare all their income sources [including you Mr. President]
- Media publicising corruption
- A judicial body to investigate corruption
- Rewards for reporting corruption if it shows to be true
- Judges are in charge of appointing senior civil service members
- A business integrity forum - to ensure businesses do not have to give bribes to people.
- Limit the amount of money businesses can give to political parties - all business may only donate to parties and not to individuals
- Employ foreigners alongside judiciary to investigate corruption
- Politicians can register to have their finances investigated by the judiciary - Establish their credentials as "clean" politicians
- Politicians including the president cannot have shares or ownership over state assets
- Establish a citizen report card - to survey citizens opinions / experiences of various state companies / state ministries. The results would be publicised in the media
- A UN workshop on corruption for politicians in a country
- A minister for corruption - drawn from civil society
- An international court in the country appointed by the AU to deal with corruption; validating elections - Reasons for this local judiciary is not skilled enough - concerns that local judiciary may not be as efficient due to lack of funding
- International police training for investigations / audits of people's finances
- Community groups - individuals joining together when seeking financing / applications for services - may reduce corruption

- NGO's can talk direct to the president about corruption
- Appointing judiciary with approval of parliament
- Simplify tax regime - a single tax for people and a single tax for businesses both over a certain level of income - This reduces scope for corruption
- The public service proposes expenditure for government and then the government decides on it
- A tracking survey - how much of government funding budgeted for schools, health clinics etc. actually reaches them - citizens monitoring the budget
- Party financing must be made public - who supported them
- Political parties must have a party support base of people | must garner at least 1,000 signatures to form a party
- Political leaders must have their finances investigated
- Party base nominates those who can become politicians after any elections
- Protect those in the civil service who expose corruption
- Media presence at court cases | especially corruption cases
- Media can have access to public service to audit where money is being "lost" along the chain of bureaucracy
- Must vote for a party rather than individual politicians - reduces corruption such as buying votes / politicians doing favours for people
- Reform within the police by the police
- Making people aware of the consequences of corruption. They will be less likely to give in to corruption or accept it
- Force new legislation on corruption by gathering votes from across the political divide in parliament

- THIRTY-FIRST STEP - POLITICS

#31 TO ERITREAN PRESIDENT ISAIAS AFEWERKI - POLITICS

31/05/2017 - 7/06/2017
TO ERITREAN PRESIDENT
Dear Ambassador,
Please can you pass the following on to President Afewerki
Dear Mr President
I have a number of suggestions for you with regard to progressing towards a more open society. Some of these ideas are innovative such as "mandate parties". In the west these would be similar to the "green party" which campaigns on a mandate to save the environment. I want your country to be a light in the dark; a beacon of hope for democracy in Africa and you are the man to do this.

- Children write letters to President Afewerki - there hopes and criticisms. Winning essays from each school are passed on to the president.
- The president cannot be a leader of a political party [can be a member of it though]
- Politicians must have certain level of education and be literate to compete in elections
- "Mandate parties" campaigning around an issue - Islam / political reform / employment / corruption etc. [Ambassador Chilcott you are going to have to talk to various politicians in Eritrea about this]
- Set up a democracy institute for Eritrea and the rest of the world
- Embassy officials of different governments can question government ministers

- THIRTY-SECOND STEP - FOURTH EMOTIONAL LETTER

#32 TO ERITREAN PRESIDENT ISAIAS AFEWERKI - FOURTH EMOTIONAL LETTER

12/07/2017 - 15/07/2017

TO ERITREAN PRESIDENT

Dear Ambassador,

Please can you pass the following on to President Afewerki

Dear Mr President

If you have been following my ideas [I hope you approve of them] Really we are talking about commitment here - to see this course to the end. You are safe if you leave office [after elections]. Democracy is not perfect but it is the best system there is right now. True happiness lies in doing good to others. You could set up your own ex-presidential fund if you leave office to do good works. Charities and NGO's are changing the world and you can be a part of that. Personally I would be happier if you do not stay on as president. There is too much association with negativity here - you have had your flaws as president - Can you openly admit that to yourself. The greatest thing you can do is hand over to a stable democracy. Are you still committed to democracy - Please be so!

- THIRTY-THIRD STEP - FREEDOM OF SPEECH

#33 TO ERITREAN PRESIDENT ISAIAS AFEWERKI - FREEDOM OF SPEECH

22/07/2017 - 21/08/2017

TO ERITREAN PRESIDENT

Dear Ambassador,

Please can you pass the following on to President Afewerki

Dear Mr President

Allow NGO's to speak at third level colleges. Allow debates in universities on anything from democracy to education. Commemorating people who have died and worked for social justice - Speeches given in universities / school halls. Your party politicians attending these meetings and assuring people they can speak out and that they are safe to do so. Politics does involve pressure on those elected; without it you would be a dictatorship. Students are the future of your country and independent thinking should be encouraged. Do you get the feeling that people are not being genuine to you - if no one can criticise you, you are a dictatorship. Is there a sharp divide between the people and politicians - their right to choose who represents them if this is so you could be described as a dictatorship. You should compare yourself to those around you other countries - how do they treat their people. How do you stand in relation to them. Do others describe you as a dictatorship - if they do then there must be substantial and committed changes. I hope when I have finished working with you that you will be one of the most democratic countries in the world. A new era for Eritrea - you might not always be president indeed no politician should ever be president for life. The typical standard abroad is two terms of seven years and then no more - if this is not so you are raising concerns about being a dictatorship.

- THIRTY-FOURTH STEP - REDUCING MILITARY BUDGET - KEEPING MILITARY BUSY

#34 TO THE CHIEF OF STAFF OF THE DEFENCE FORCES - REDUCING MILITARY BUDGET - KEEPING MILITARY BUSY

18/09/2017 - 16/10/2017

TO ERITREAN PRESIDENT

Dear Ambassador,

Ambassador Chilcott - If Eritrea moves towards a democracy - its military spending will be significantly reduced. There is the danger of a coup d'etat [It has happened many times in other African countries at this stage]. So the strategy here is to keep the military busy - by involving them in UN peacekeeping missions. Also by engaging in international military training for the Eritrean army. This also helps end the isolation of Eritrea in the world - a priority.

Dear Sir, I think your president is moving towards a democracy - Now in other countries particularly in Africa when the power of the military is reduced in many cases a coup d'etat erupts. This should not be so for Eritrea - A responsible military must recognise that it cannot be involved in politics. You have important responsibility in ensuring peace is maintained - no matter who is president [elections]. Soldiers are brave people. They would follow your orders [keep the peace]. In some cases the military is a business such as in the USA that is not good. Asking you to accept cuts in your budget is necessary as you make peace with the countries around you. More resources can be spent on your people as a result. Generally where the military does not exercise too much power - you have stable governments and like my own country more can be spent on looking after the people. One area of suggestion is that Eritrea contribute peacekeeping forces to the UN. Keeping the peace [again] only this time in another country. Generally other countries in the wealthier west contribute to the costs of such operations so there is no danger of the government reducing aid assistance to your people to support the military. You could also become involved in joint military training with a country in the west

- THIRTY-FIFTH STEP - APOLOGY

#35 TO ERITREAN PRESIDENT ISAIAS AFEWERKI - APOLOGY

23/10/2017
TO ERITREAN PRESIDENT
Dear Ambassador,
Everyone knows that you have been involved in proxy wars both now and in the past in Sudan, Ethiopia and Eritrea. I will say this - these are attempts at power. You have to make a decision which you want friends or power. Power equals many enemies; continued fighting; an economy that is severely damaged. Friends equals not interfering inside another country [they would probably reciprocate on this issue - they need to] A really difficult and hard thing to do is to apologise for wrongdoings - but you might be surprised to see other countries making the same apology to you. It is all a question of who is willing to move first on the issue. You would gain many friends - again I remind you the choice you make is between friends and power.

- THIRTY-SIXTH STEP - MEDIA RIGHTS / LAWS

#36 TO ERITREAN PRESIDENT ISAIAS AFEWERKI - MEDIA RIGHTS / LAWS

20/11/2017 - 25/12/2017
TO ERITREAN PRESIDENT
Dear Ambassador,
Please can you pass the following on to President Afewerki
Dear Mr President
What do you think of the following suggestions for media laws and policy. I think your country could become very open-minded and tolerant. With free press governments would be more stable and have greater integrity - The press would ensure this. You are at the beginning of a new era for your country. Your people will be happier and unafraid to express their opinions. You have to admit your country is a very closed state when it comes to the media. You would if you compared yourself to other countries both in the region and in the west. There is work to be done here!

MEDIA RIGHTS

- Media can criticise the president / government
- Must be respect for religion in media - A right of response for religious in media
- Right of response for government to media articles
- Allow in foreign media outlets such as the BBC Worldservice
- Eritrean media can have branches in other countries
- Journalists may have access to detailed accounts of government spending

Laws And Libel Laws

- A centre of journalists, religious, business, university professors to draw up media laws
- Incitement to hatred between different ethnic groups must be against the law
- Respect for religion provided it is not extreme
- Journalists must not be censored for expressing an opinion
- Parliamentary cross-party committees on investigations into journalists being persecuted / killed
- In libel laws burden of proof must lie with the complainant rather than the journalist
- One third of broadcasting licenses must go to community media
- Cannot refer to ethnic identities within the media
- A human rights commission to regulate journalism
- No businesses can control more than 10% of the media

Purpose of Media

- To hold officials to account by acting as a "watchdog" that brings misuses of power or policy failures to the knowledge of the public
- To provide citizens with the information they need to participate in society
- To serve as a forum for different views both official and alternative - to mobilise support for a cause
- The media must be a moral agency
- The role of the media is to expand knowledge and overcome biases

Media Diversity

- Newspapers can publish contradictory articles journalists on each side taking a side on an issue
- In elections newspapers television must publish the goals of all political parties as they are written
- Political party assemblies to ensure that party political policies are more than just a rubberstamp for leaders
- A "nationwide" programme to highlight good works being done all around the country
- A Reuters style news agency for Eritrea - government financed - run by national journalists union - insist on factual / accurate news reporting from the agency
- Allow public relations companies

Corruption

- There must be a separation between media ownership and editorial decision-making

- To deal with bribes in journalism - journalists can look for support from editors
- Media assistance body to deal with corruption in journalism

LAST STEP - NEGOTIATORS GOING BEFORE PARLIAMENT AND EXPLAINING DECISIONS

TO ERITREAN PRESIDENT ISAIAS AFEWERKI - NEGOTIATORS GOING BEFORE PARLIAMENT AND EXPLAINING DECISIONS

12/03/2018

TO ERITREAN PRESIDENT

Dear Ambassador,

Please can you pass the following on to President Afewerki

Dear Mr President

With regard to drawing up a new constitution you are going to have to involve all political parties on this including regional parties. This should be done in conjunction with a civil society assembly making proposals which I hope politicians accept. In fact civil society should lead on this. Negotiators of the new constitution [civil society leaders and political negotiators] should then go before parliament and explain their decisions

SYRIA

Purpose : To persuade President Bashar to retire and allow a successor to negotiate with the Syrian opposition and rebels. To persuade the rebels not to seek revenge and not to pursue an extremist version of Islam for Syria.

Strategy : Make Mr Bashar realise that staying on will result in too much bloodshed, that even if he wins the international community will not accept him. Empowering him by making it as easy as possible for him to choose to step down - "You have friends .. tell them what you want to see done if you step down" "You can choose who takes your place and negotiates with the rebels" "You need not worry over Al-Qaeda taking over the rebels the international community will not let that happen" Asking him "Would you be prepared to step down if it was the only way to end the bloodshed" Pointing out "We all need to focus on the suffering".

KEYWORDS

"President Bashar Al Assad" "Rotating Presidency" "Red Crescent" "Syrian Army" "Syrian Minister Of Commerce And Technology Dr. Imad Sabouni" "Elections" "Ceasefire" "Imaam" "Geneva Talks" "Syrian National Coalition" "Free Syrian Army" "Shia" "Sunnis" "Russia" "USA" "Turkish Foreign Minister Ahmet Davutoglu" "OIC" "Saudi Arabia" "Iran"

24/06/2014 PAUL ARMSTRONG - GET ADVICE PRESIDENT ASSAD

24/06/2014

TO THE BAATH PARTY SYRIA

Dear Sir / Madam,

Can you pass the following on to President Assad,

Dear Mr Assad

This suffering is not going to end until you talk to the rebels directly – YOU – along with your friends in Iran. I believe the Koran does talk about meeting with your enemy. Mohammed was a really good guy in his time and I don't think he would be happy with what is going on in Iraq and your country. If any statement holds weight it is that Mohammed in heaven is not happy. You are all brothers you are all Muslims. There is a way to get peace THERE IS. The bottom line is that more people are going to die; more people are going to loose their limbs, more children are going to loose their parents. Already you have set up a legacy of division and anger and hatred. This war is not going to end in a week or a month. God / Allah does cry and right now he is crying for your country. What can you do – You are the President – how are you going to end the fighting and bring peace? I would trust other peacemakers / Muslim peacemakers from your region get their advice. Lakhdar Brahimi is hopeless so I would skip him. STICK AT THIS DO NOT CHANGE YOUR MIND.

3/06/2014 PAUL ARMSTRONG - THINKING ABOUT PEACE IN SYRIA

03/06/2014

TO THE GARDAI

Dear Sir / Madam,

please can you pass this on to the Garda Commissioner. I hope you are aware of my previous emails on this topic [in particular the idea of a rotating presidency. You can check out my ideas on Syria at http://www.peace-implementation.info/syria_peace_proposal.pdf - Syria Peace Proposal

 TO THE GARDAI – I NEED YOUR HELP – CAN YOU GET IRAN AND IRAQ AND SAUDI ARABIA TO READ THIS EMAIL]

What is peace? It is no fighting with rebels; a compromised agreement where all sides make real concessions [concessions they have not been prepared to make in the past]. It means saying the other side are a relevant and recognisable partner which you have to work with. THIS IS ALWAYS WHAT PEACE IS. What are the big issues? The rebels want a new president; perhaps changes in Islamic Law. Getting the international community to join together to promote peace from all sides. Getting all sides to recognise a new president won from across the country [I am sure you would think it fair that rebel areas could vote in a presidential election. So how are you going to do that? Your government is going to have to have regular contacts with the rebels [there can be an intermediary]. There has to be a ceasefire. You need outside help – the international community should be united in making you both talk about a real lasting ceasefire. Ceasefire is a confidence building measure – It says both of you are really committed to peace. YOU ARE GOING TO HAVE TO STRUCTURE PEACE HERE – ceasefire comes first. What's next – take the easy steps first – allowing free movement of humanitarian aid across border lines; exchange of prisoners; Allowing a small number of mediators to monitor conflict lines [from Islamic countries]. Who is on your side? The rebels can have people siding with them from the international community so can you AND these people are party to the peace talks – ACTUALLY AT THE NEGOTIATING TABLE WITH EACH SIDE. You need to reformat the way peace talks are held. Keep it local – I would exclude Russia and the USA – Let the OIC hold the talks – They are Muslims like you – Russia and the USA are too divided. How do I deal with common problems ? You are both making ultimatums. You are refusing to recognise the other side. You are both refusing to talk to certain people. First break is each side CAN and is allowed to choose who they send to contact meetings and who talks for them at each stage. A courageous step by Assad would be to acknowledge that the rebels do have people in the community who represent them [REMEMBER if you are going for peace peace actions and ideas This means weakening your own side – becoming vulnerable – taking a risk]. Are you prepared to become vulnerable and risk things for peace. A courageous move by the rebels would be to say Bashar could be president again [in elections that are held across the country]. The talks held previously did not work - there were too many players – both sides leading the talks were making statements they should not have said. Local countries are more likely to negotiate successfully. So who to choose – I would choose Iraq [neutral] Saudi Arabia [Pro-Rebels] and Iran [pro-Assad]. Are you prepared to accept election results that are held NATIONWIDE Assad. To the rebels are you prepared to implement a ceasefire before talks. The Crunch Issue. The presidency is the crunch issue – Assad there will be no peace unless this issue is resolved. There will have to be another round of voting to include areas held by rebels [and Assad areas]. There will only be peace if all sides have had their say in voting. What could happen? This is what I fear for – Assad wins elections in areas controlled by government forces. Rebels refuse to accept the elections as a sham. Fighting continues – more people are displaced and killed – more infrastructure is destroyed. Talks fail at Geneva because each side refuses to agree with the other on what to talk about and who should be included in the talks. I fear that the wounds of this war will take generations to heal. There will continue to be international trade sanctions. The whole region of the middle east will be divided on Syria and stay that way. Realisations Even if and this is unlikely in the short to medium term rebels are defeated what might happen is continued violence with rebels changing their tactics to terrorist style actions – such as car bombings; suicide attacks; assassinations. The violence is NOT going to end this way – the way things are going right now. To Assad winning the presidency in government held areas means nothing for peace. MY MANTRA : My mantra should be – I will take risks that are scary for me; I will make positive statements for peace; I will say everything is negotiable; Saudi Arabia – Iraq – and Iran are going to have to work together and accept that ANYONE CAN END UP BEING PRESIDENT.

04/2014 PAUL ARMSTRONG - PEACE PROPOSAL FOR SYRIA -

04/2014

TO RELEVANT PEACEMAKERS

- First their is a ceasefire. Then there is an exchange of prisoners and medicine
- Coordinate peace statements on both sides
- Syrian president takes a big risk and acknowledges he will have to talk to Syrian rebel representatives and that nobody is excluded - "You can't make peace with your friends - If you want peace you must talk to your enemies"
- Inform Iran of peace ideas
- Get a religious scholar from Egypt as high up as possible [Religious scholars are respected to advise Syrian rebels and lead them to peace

- President Assad agrees to a rotating presidency for six months. Then a person chosen by the Syrian rebels but not part of them to lead presidency for another six months. After this there would be presidential elections - In which Bashar may participate

- A vice president from someone outside Syrian rebels chosen by them to be in Syrian government until changeover and vice versa

- Stress the suffering must end - all sides must agree on this

- Exchange of prisoners

- Iran / Turkey / Saudia Arabia / Iraq increase substantially aid to Syrian red crescent

- Contacting donors to reaassure you they will help rebuild your country if their is successful talks

- A UN team must assess the damage in Syria

- No target zones where people can go [Villages] that are not strategically important to either side behind their lines

- Start a commission representing all sides in Syria / Of Syrians to talk to both sides and bring them together

- Ask the question is up for discussion - how?

- Disarmament of rebels is up for discussion - but how?

- What is the biggest concession you are prepared to make[both sides]

- How are you going to guarantee implementation of the peace plan

- Acknowledge the Syrian army must remain - their can be a few changes in positions at and near the top

- THE STRATEGY IS :

  - Realising the destruction that has been caused - making both sides want to end the fighting

- Direct talks [use the famous quote above ...]

- Both sides acknowledge the presidency is the core issue - How are we going to deal with it ?

- Discussing standard issues that are easy to deal wtih

- Making the point - unless both sides make BIG concessions there will be no peace - This is the only way peace has ever been achieved

- Discussing the standard issue of implementation and enforcing agreement

- Pragmatism - Syria needs a stable army

- Stress to them this is how things could be - use the word could a lot

----

18/02/2014 PAUL ARMSTRONG - PEACE IN SYRIA - ROTATING PRESIDENCY

18/02/2014|

TO UK PRIME MINISTER DAVID CAMERON

Dear Ambassador Chilcott,

I have a proposal for peace in Syria. I propose a rotating presidency for Syria over the next 18 months – 9 months for Bashar Al Assad. Then another president for nine months [someone chosen by the rebels from civil society but not someone who is a direct member of the rebel movement] After that there would be elections in which President Bashar may run for presidency again if he chooses. I sent the email below to the Syrian ministry of commerce and technology [Minister Dr. Imad Sabouni] for President Bashar Al Assad. In it I ask the President to get directly involved in peace talks.

TO DR IMAD SABOUNI - 18/02/2014 - PAUL ARMSTRONG - PRESIDENT BASHAR AL ASSAD ATTENDING TALKS

18/02/2014

TO SYRIAN MINISTER OF COMMERCE AND TECHNOLOGY DR. IMAD SABOUNI

[PLEASE LET MR SABOUNI READ THIS EMAIL]

Dear Mr Sabouni

[I hope you understand english :-)]

Will you pass the following on to President Bashar Al Assad. It may help the Geneva Peace talks if the president chooses to get involved directly in them himself. He can make better decisions AND he will be aware of what everyone is thinking and saying directly. He would be able to make executive decisions on the spot. Sometimes having a leader present adds more weight to the negotiations. His negotiators cannot make decisions without him. The peace process make work faster and better. I will say this the president choosing to attend the talks means he will be making difficult decisions – He will feel more responsible this is the nature of negotiations. There will be a peace agreement – repeatedly there have been conflicts that looked like they could not be resolved but they were. IT IS THE BEST DECISION THE PRESIDENT CAN MAKE TO

ATTEND THE TALKS HIMSELF. To quote someone "If we are not talking to President Bashar Al Assad we should be".

2/02/2014 PAUL ARMSTRONG - TO PRIME MINISTER DAVID CAMERON - INCLUDING PRESIDENT ASSAD IN TALKS

02/02/2014

TO UK PRIME MINISTER DAVID CAMERON

Dear Ambassador Chilcott,

Please can you pass this on to Prime Minister David Cameron.

Dear Mr Cameron,

The peace talks in Syria are not going to work as they are. You are going to have to get President Assad involved in the talks – present at them – If he is made responsible for what is happening – made to meet the other side there will be more progress. Make the rebels realise this [There will be more progress if he is involved] You have a few bad people out there [its] Lakhdar, Kerry, etc. but on a positive note there is no more gambling [peace would have happened alot sooner if there had not been before now]. I will write to Bashar myself – patience and persistence may work. My personal strategy is to persuade him to step down now and choose to run in the next presidential elections as a candidate. You may check out my website to see all my correspondence to him www.peace-implementation.info/syria_key_ideas.html

02/02/2014 PAUL ARMSTRONG - TO SYRIAN PRESIDENT BASHAR AL-ASSAD - WHAT SHOULD YOU DO?

02/02/2014

TO SYRIAN PRESIDENT BASHAR AL ASSAD

Dear President Assad,

I hope you get this letter. You are going to have to put peace first ahead of your own status PLEASE. What future would you like for your country. Things are getting worse on all sides. There is infighting among the rebels, your country is being destroyed – infrastructure that will take years to rebuild. If you win what do you win? I have seen peace talks before that have failed in other countries – they fail because each side refuses to make any REAL sacrifice refuses to do something BIG anything that would go OVER their "red lines". What are your sides red lines? What real sacrifices to you refuse to make? what big actions do you refuse to make? I will ask the same thing of the rebels. I have talked to you before about this – There seems to me to be only one choice you can make – to choose to "temporarily" step down until next presidential elections. Think about it. Would it end the fighting? I will also write to the rebel side.

2/02/2014 PAUL ARMSTRONG - TO SYRIAN NATIONAL COALITION - NEGOTIATIONS - PRAGMATIC AND REALISTIC

02/02/2014
TO SYRIAN NATIONAL COALITION

Dear Sarah,
Please can you pass this on to the right people in the Syrian rebellion. You are going to have to make some REAL compromises for peace. I have seen peace talks before that have failed in other countries – they fail because each side refuses to make any REAL sacrifice refuses to do something BIG anything that would go OVER their "red lines". You are going to have to talk to Mr Assad [don't act on PRINCIPLES put peace first]. It may take a few weeks of negotiations to come to a deal – stick at the talks – DON'T GIVE UP. You have friends and they will help you – Be pragmatic and realistic.

26/07/2013 PAUL ARMSTRONG - TO PRESIDENT BASHAR AL-ASSAD - HOPE FOR PEACE

26/07/2013
TO PRESIDENT BASHAR AL ASSAD - VIA SYRIAN PARLIAMENT [Contact Form]

Dear Sirs,
Please can you let President Assad read this.
Dear Mr Assad,
You can run for elections in 2014. You are going to have to compromise though – if there is going to be any settlement – if there is any hope for peace – You will have to retire from office for now. I am genuine about you running for elections again and that means – you stay in the country if you want. Your government is going to have to talk to the opposition and work out a plan for peace WORKING TOGETHER. Right now the violence is drawing in extremists on all sides. The rebels do not necessarily take over power either – there has to be some sort of council – they can appoint members to this council though. I would get as broad a spectrum of members involved in this

council as possible. The rebels will have to say that yes in any free elections anyone including you can run for election.

Thank You

TO PRESIDENT BASHAR AL ASSAD - VIA SYRIAN PARLIAMENT - 30-05-2013

30/05/2013

TO PRESIDENT BASHAR AL ASSAD - VIA SYRIAN PARLIAMENT [Contact Form]

Please pass the following on to the President. I want to end the violence now. I have some ideas for peace and the conference must go ahead. This violence is escalating. Now you have Hezbollah working for you Now the rebels will be receiving weapons from Europe. There will be no future for your country if this continues - we are talking about a lot more bloodshed. What needs to be done ? There has to be a ceasefire - If you stop fighting I am pretty sure the rebels will stop too. All issues are eventually on the table when the conference is held. Ask for advice [internationally - UN etc.] on how to hold a ceasefire | how to maintain peace along a peace line between your two forces. I am not happy about the sectarian massacres. I am not accusing you directly but they have been carried out. You could state publicly that you acknowledge they may have been carried out and will investigate and punish those found guilty of this crime. That would help peace. The issues that people want to talk about have to be talked about. NO MORE BLOODSHED PLEASE!

30/05/2013 PAUL ARMSTRONG - TO NATIONAL COALITION OF SYRIAN REVOLUTION AND OPPOSITION FORCES - A SUGGESTION

30/05/2013

TO NATIONAL COALITION OF SYRIAN REVOLUTION AND OPPOSITION FORCES

Dear Sirs,

This is just a suggestion. I hope you find it helpful. An Imam can run as leader of a village / town / city / region appointed by a religious council or appointed by key figures in society.

God Bless You / Allah Bless You

27/05/2013 PAUL ARMSTRONG - TO PRESIDENT BARACK OBAMA - PEACE IN SYRIA - IDEAS FOR GENEVA TALKS

27/05/2013

TO US PRESIDENT BARACK OBAMA

Dear Mr Bazarnic,

Please can you pass the following on to President Barack Obama directly. I include ideas for the Geneva Talks conference in June as well as an email I sent to President Bashar Al Assad [through his US embassy]. Thank You.

Dear Mr President,

Ideas For The Geneva Talks :

- Talks should be in stages – with goals to be achieved at each stage
- Give them work to do at the conference
- There has to be a democracy – define general structures
- Rebuild country – How to do this ?
- Relations with other countries
- Religious laws – Sharia laws – What level ?
- How to decide leader ?
- Include political / civil society / opposition / rebels all together – They decide together whether Bashar should step down
- A further conference to decide this
- Can appoint an interim leader until elections
- [I am hopeful both sides will accept the idea of a conference of all parties to decide on the fate of Bashar]

27/05/2013 PAUL ARMSTRONG - TO SYRIAN PRESIDENT BASHAR AL ASSAD - PEACE IN SYRIA

Dear Ambassador,

Please can you pass the following on to President Bashar Al Assad.

Thank You.

Dear Mr Assad,

I am glad that you are committed to taking part in the Geneva Talks. I hope this will mean an end to the violence. What I want to say is you should be prepared to entertain the possibility that you will not be the leader of Syria after all negotiations.

There is a lot of work to be done in these negotiations. You have to talk about how to transform your country into a democracy, rebuilding your country and so on and a mechanism for deciding on how to decide the status of leader of the country.

27/05/2013 PAUL ARMSTRONG - TO SYRIAN PRESIDENT BASHAR AL ASSAD - PEACE IN SYRIA

27/05/2013

TO SYRIAN PRESIDENT BASHAR AL ASSAD

Dear Ambassador,

Please can you pass the following on to President Bashar Al Assad.

Thank You.

Dear Mr Assad,

I am glad that you are committed to taking part in the Geneva Talks. I hope this will mean an end to the violence. What I want to say is you should be prepared to entertain the possibility that you will not be the leader of Syria after all negotiations. There is a lot of work to be done in these negotiations. You have to talk about how to transform your country into a democracy, rebuilding your country and so on and a mechanism for deciding on how to decide the status of leader of the country.

17/05/2013 PAUL ARMSTRONG - PEACE IN SYRIA - TO FOREIGN MINISTER AHMET DAVUTOGLU

17/05/2013

TO TURKISH FOREIGN MINISTER AHMET DAVUTOGLU

Dear Ambassador,

I am asking you to pass the following two messages on to Foreign Minister Ahmet Davutoglu. The first one I want him to pass on to the Syrian National Coalition at their meeting with him in Istanbul on May 23rd. [Even if he does not pass on this message he is free to use the ideas contained in it] The second one I hope he can pass on to President Bashar Al Assad of Syria. [This one I would like him to pass on as it is written]

[TO THE SYRIAN NATIONAL COALITION – THE FREE SYRIAN ARMY]

Dear Sirs,

The violence has to end – there must be stability. I am concerned about growing sectarian tensions between Shia and Sunnis – I want to prevent this now. I want to ensure there is no religious war. I am also concerned that your organisation might splinter into sub-groups at some stage a reason to negotiate now. There will be no more carnage after a peace agreement – This agreement will be final. I believe it is more than possible that Mr Assad will resign. I advise you to accept during negotiations that you will accept some members of Mr Assad's regime in any new government. Mr Assad himself does not have to be at the talks and probably will not be. I recommend that each side nominate three countries to be involved taking part in negotiations along with Russia and the USA. If there is no conference there may be far more suffering than you expect. I want to tell you after the negotiations all countries will be united in wanting to help rebuild your country. A positive aspect of the negotiations is that you will have a strong advocate on your side during the talks – the US who have repeatedly said that they want Mr Assad to go. However I wish to point out for the sake of peace Mr Assad's position must be vague at the start – he will not say "I Resign Now" but with negotiations I am confident this will happen.

Thank You For Your Time

[TO PRESIDENT BASHAR AL ASSAD]

Dear Mr Assad,

The bloodshed has to end – The people must come first. There is no point in negotiations unless they are substantive in nature. I want you to say to yourself "I cannot guarantee I will stay on as president at the end of these negotiations". I believe the Syrian National Coalition will come to the negotiations and negotiate in good faith. I recommend that each side nominate three countries to be involved in taking part in the negotiations along with Russia and the USA. If negotiations do not happen I fear there may be far more bloodshed than either side expects.

Thank You For Your Time

29/04/2013 PAUL ARMSTRONG - PEACE IN SYRIA - TO SYRIAN PRESIDENT BASHAR AL ASSAD

29/04/2013

TO SYRIAN PRESIDENT BASHAR AL-ASSAD

Dear Ambassador,

Please, please let President Assad read this.

Dear Mr Assad,

I am concerned about how things could turn out. 1. Is that the war goes on with neither side winning = more suffering for the general population / more refugees. 2. The rebels win after a long protracted fight in which extremists which are beginning to take hold now come do dominate the fighters and thus control the future of Syria. 3. The US attacks your country forcing a defeat of your army and you end up being taken prisoner by the rebel army and end up being executed. 4. The rebels win but there is serious and increasing hostilities between Sunni's / Shia's and Christians in your country leading to a new civil war – a possible Afghan scenario. It does not have to be like this! I don't want you to die and I don't want any more suffering. Time is running out. If you would put your country first then please retire – appoint someone to negotiate with the rebels. The international community has to work with the rebels – work to contain the extremist elements in it. If you leave ALL sides will be united in working for peace in Syria.

16/04/2013 PAUL ARMSTRONG - TO SYRIAN PRESIDENT BASHAR AL ASSAD - PEACE IN SYRIA

16/04/2013

TO SYRIAN PRESIDENT BASHAR AL-ASSAD

Dear Ambassador,

Please can you pass this on to President Bashar Al-Assad.

Dear Mr Assad,

Eventually you are going to be defeated. If this is a fight to the last – you will die and your supporters will fight to the last too. There has to be a negotiated settlement. Things are just getting worse and worse can you accept that. I made a suggestion and I will make it again – i ask you to retire and for a person of your choosing – YOUR choosing to take over and talk to the rebels . This is really the only hope for peace. This is the only way you are going to end the bloodshed. Can you accept the rebels are never going to talk to you. They are never going to accept you as president can you accept this too. What is your contribution to peace ? Retire – Appoint someone to talk to the rebels – Save Syria from chaos [Becoming like Afghanistan And there are concerns that if there is not a negotiated settlement that this is the way Syria could turn out]. The critical thing here is that I do not want Syria to end up like Afghanistan did – You have to retire | There must be negotiations.

22/02/2013 PAUL ARMSTRONG - TO SYRIAN PRESIDENT BASHAR AL-ASSAD - PROPOSALS FOR PEACE

22/02/2013

TO SYRIAN PRESIDENT BASHAR AL-ASSAD

Dear Ambassador,

Please can you pass the following on to Syrian President Bashar Al Assad.

Dear Mr Assad,

I have a few suggestions for peace. I suggest you propose sending vice-president Farouk al-Shara to talks with the Syrian opposition along with others of your choice while still being president. The peace proposal can be developed / negotiated – you do have capable negotiators. The war has gone on for nearly two years now – this is too long. That means you have to talk. It is a war of attrition yes – but right now the rebels appear to be making some gains. Both your side and the rebels have their backers so this is not going to end. You can say I will accept the results of the negotiations even if it means me having to retire. A third-party country could offer you asylum.

May Allah Bless Your Country With Peace

10/02/2013 PAUL ARMSTRONG - TO PRESIDENT ASSAD - PEACE IN SYRIA

10/02/2013

TO SYRIAN PRESIDENT BASHAR AL-ASSAD

Dear Ambassador,

Please can you pass the following on to President Assad as soon as possible.

Dear Mr Assad,

Both sides could offer cantonment of troops – I don't think disarmament is viable at this stage REALISTICALLY SPEAKING. There needs to be gestures for peace at the start. Release of women prisoners will not harm you – they would be cantoning troops and this is a bigger risk for them. There has to be intermediaries [a security force] between your two sides – it does not have to be large just enough to keep the peace. You could say you would retire if that turns out to be the will of the people in a referendum – "I RESPECT THE WILL OF THE PEOPLE". Your friends want peace AND I think that what is happening now is the best chance for peace. Release the women prisoners PLEASE. Someone has to start the peace process. You can go to Russia or Iran and have them host the peace talks – I think Al Khatib would be in favour of this – would you too?

07/02/2013 PAUL ARMSTRONG - PEACE IN SYRIA

7/02/2013

TO SYRIAN PRESIDENT BASHAR AL ASSAD

Dear Mr Hisham,

I am writing to you asking you to pass this on to ambassador Isolde Moylan for him to communicate this email to President Bashar Al Assad. Can you do this immediately? Can you confirm that you have sent on this email?

Dear Mr Assad,

The offer by Mr Al-Khatib is an opening. You do not know where this is going to go but it is worth a shot. Do you want peace – this is an opportunity here. It is not a difficult concession to say you will release the women prisoners – The story of peace is that people make gestures for peace – they may cease fighting if you do. They want to talk with vice-president Mr Farouk Al-Shara – how about you both talk to them?? You can do it directly or indirectly through mediators. Your hold on the presidency must not be concrete – you must say to yourself I am prepared willing to retire – maybe a referendum on whether you should stay on. The Syrian opposition is going to have to be given some power before a referendum – This will be difficult – A government council running the country with you still as president until a referendum. It is going to have to be quick though a referendum – You are going to have to name a date during mediation talks – not more than four months away. Your friends in Iran and other Muslim countries can oversee and vouch that the referendum was fair.

Sincerely

This is a really good chance for peace!!

17/01/2013 PAUL ARMSTRONG - TO SYRIAN PRESIDENT BASHAR AL-ASSAD - PEACE IN SYRIA

17/01/2013

TO SYRIAN PRESIDENT BASHAR AL-ASSAD

Dear Ambassador,

Please can you pass the following on to President Bashar Al-Assad.

Dear Mr Assad,

Peace is the objective. The rebels are relevant because they are not going away – they won't disappear. Most members fighting you – they are Syrians – your own people. Ask yourself why did they take up arms? – because they are not looking for personal power [leadership of the country]. A lot of people both in the country and in the Diaspora [people from Syria living abroad] - I would say ALL of the Diaspora want change - check it out – check the media coverage – Those interviewed by international media who were from Syria have all called for a transition which would include you retiring. You are completely focused on the fighting that is where you are at. You are completely focused on the fighting that is where you are at. You should ask yourself the questions – Should I stop fighting? Am I going to succeed easily or this going to be a very long bloody war with too many deaths? How is the international community going to treat me even if I win after a war? How am I going to rebuild my country after a war if I win – because I will most likely not receive international aid for anything other than humanitarian assistance? So I am being pragmatic you are not – I know what needs to be done – the fighting must end And this is not going to happen if you stay. Do you accept that? You were going to retire before – there could have been peace then. If you retired : Am I right - would there be peace? would there be a transitional government? would the international community including Iran and Russia look after your country? would there be reform? is this the only way to peace that would include everyone?

8/1/2013 PAUL ARMSTRONG - AN TAOISEACH - PEACE IN SYRIA

8/01/2013

TO AN TAOISEACH - ENDA KENNY

An Taoiseach,

Can you see that the following email gets passed on to Syrian President Bashar Al-Assad.

Dear Mr Bashar,

You are feeling like a real leader – I saw the chanting the arms raised at your recent speech and you spoke about the bloodshed. But you are only offering more war and no solution that would include all parties. When I deal with peace I deal with pragmatism – what will work. My priorities are ending the bloodshed 1. – This means all parties stop fighting Realistically this is not going to happen as long as you are there 2. – You were not a democracy – there were restricted parties / restrictions on freedom of expression. So there must be a convention where all parties sit down and decide the future of Syria. I am asking you to resign – There are two options here 1. The status quo which means continued fighting OR 2. You retire and negotiations on the future of Syria WOULD HAPPEN! -- That is really it -- IF YOU GO THERE WILL BE PEACE! Your government will talk to the rebels – the rebels and the Syrian National Council and the opposition will sit down and talk THAT IS WHAT WILL HAPPEN if you go. The question is which do you want to hold on to power or peace. It is not easy to resign – I know but you will save a lot of lives if you do. God is not happy with people dying as they are.

30/12/2012 PAUL ARMSTRONG - TO THE SYRIAN NATIONAL COUNCIL + FREE SYRIAN ARMY

30/12/2012
TO SYRIAN NATIONAL COUNCIL

Dear Sir,

Please read this and pass it on to the Free Syrian Army [including all members of it] Thank You.

Dear Sirs,

You need help big time – Bashar is probably leaving. Your first priority has to be a stable government. Bashar will probably appoint someone else to take over from him to negotiate with you. Negotiate with this person [There is definite change here]. You need to deal with arms – fighters should hand over their weapons to their leaders and these should then be disposed of. I would not hold a grudge against the Syrian army – in fact I think the army is crucial to peace in the future of Syria – PRAGMATISM here. A constitution – Islamic law should hold equal influence with Democratic law this is a realistic compromise. There must be no revenge – There must be no revenge or you will plunge the country into disorder – every fighter must realise this. You need help from your neighbours – Iran / Saudi Arabia / Turkey. An international fund to help rebuild your country. I have some ideas on employment generation strategies you may check them out at www.peace-implementation.info/employment_ideas.html . I would respect the leadership that exists in the Free Syrian army and in the Syrian National Council – again disorder would result if you do not. To Al-Nusra I would say you can continue your practice of Islam and lobbying government on Islamic law but you must respect the will of the people and of government. Mohamed never forced anyone against their will – Remain true to him.

P.S. It is worth checking out the weblink : -)

24/12/2012 PAUL ARMSTRONG - TO SYRIAN PRESIDENT BASHAR AL-ASSAD - PEACE IN SYRIA

24/12/2012
TO SYRIAN PRESIDENT BASHAR AL-ASSAD

Dear Ambassador,

Please can you pass the following on to Syrian President Bashar Al-Assad.

Dear Mr Assad,

You are not going to defeat the Free Syrian Army that is for certain and they are not going to negotiate with you. So this is going to be a long conflict. Your vice-president has said neither side is going to win. If there were talks between your side and the rebels I do not think you could stay on. I think Mr Brahimi the UN envoy said once that there needs to be fundamental change in the leadership. This is realism about what is possible. You probably do not like me for saying so often that you should leave [I will tell you I do not want you to be defeated; I do not want you to die; I want peace;] You are angry because everyone is trying to force you – but YOU ARE in the middle of a war and there is bloodshed and this is going to continue for a long while – For too long! Do you think I am right that maybe you should leave – IF THIS IS THE ONLY WAY THE BLOODSHED WOULD END! Do you want the bloodshed to end? Are you prepared to ask yourself the question would I leave? The future is not certain but some things will happen no matter what you do. What do you want for Syria and not for you? I know you have friends in the world. Talk to the Russians; talk to the Iranians your friends tell them if I leave I want you to ensure the following for my country's future. You may have some justifiable concerns about some of the rebels who have links to Al-Qaeda but I feel the international community will ensure what they would like does not succeed. Thank you for reading this email.

Sincerely

WOULD I LEAVE?

21/12/2012 PAUL ARMSTRONG - TO SYRIAN NATIONAL COUNCIL - PASS ON TO AL NUSRA FRONT

21/12/2012

TO SYRIAN NATIONAL COUNCIL

Dear Sir,

Please can you pass the following on to the leaders of Al-Nusra front.

Dear Sirs,

Okay I will say it plain out – I do not want extremism and I do not want anarchy. Islam is a good religion AND I am a Christian saying that! You are going to have to work together – YOU – THE SYRIAN NATIONAL COUNCIL – THE FREE SYRIAN ARMY. Peace comes first – you are going to have to find a balance between your different views. There are other Islamist states in the world and they do not force strict rules on people – such as Iran. You can have a state that says Islamic law is equally important to democratic law – That is what I would reach for. My biggest concern once Bashar is gone [hopefully he will choose to leave AND the bloodshed end] is that the country would continue to be unstable: AGAIN work together – that means everyone: the democratic opposition in Syria; freedom fighters; the Syrian National Council. If Bashar leaves – someone will be left in charge after him and if this happens you will be able to negotiate a peaceful change in Syria.

GOD BLESS / ALLAH BLESS YOU

Sincerely
ISLAM IS A GOOD RELIGION!

21/12/2012 - PAUL ARMSTRONG - TO SYRIAN PRESIDENT BASHAR AL-ASSAD

21/12/2012

TO SYRIAN PRESIDENT BASHAR AL-ASSAD

Dear Ambassador,

Please can you pass the following on to president Bashar Al-Assad. PLEASE!

Dear Mr President,

Bashar how much bloodshed do you want? You are almost right "If I go none of Syria remains" actually if you do not go none of Syria may remain. Listen there is just too much destruction going on. I would be sickened by the violence if I saw what was happening on the front line. Are you prepared to sink Syria. Here is what I want – PEACE; DEMOCRACY; A PEACEFUL HANDOVER OF POWER; NO ISLAMIST EXTREMISM TAKING OVER THE COUNTRY; AN END TO ALL FIGHTING. Bashar I am telling you; you need to leave. I fear anarchy if you do not resign and leave. I have given you advice in the past as to what to do.

Sincerely

PLEASE!

15/12/2012 - PAUL ARMSTRONG - TO SYRIAN PRESIDENT BASHAR AL-ASSAD

15/12/2012

TO SYRIAN PRESIDENT BASHAR AL-ASSAD

Dear Ambassador,

Please can you pass this on to President Bashar Al-Assad as soon as possible.

Dear Mr Assad,

I know it may be difficult to choose to leave – You do not have to make any big announcements to the press. You can do it privately. I hope by now a country has offered you and your family asylum. Leave on a good note. Appoint power to someone else – someone who will talk to ALL the opposition elements. You are going to loose if you stay and there would be more bloodshed on that path. You can have your own life with your family. Your life is not over. It is a little difficult to do this – but when you do it – it is easier than you think. No one is going to say you can't or mock you in your government.

3/12/2012 - PAUL ARMSTRONG - TO AN TAOISEACH - RE: PEACE IN SYRIA

3/12/2012

TO IRISH TAOISEACH - ENDA KENNY

An Taoiseach,

I sent the email below to the Syrian embassy in the UK asking them to pass on to their president Bashar Al-Assad. I hope it helps. A suggestion : A small concession from the west may open the door to persuading him to retire to another country : I would recommend that the west states publically that it would allow neighbouring countries in the middle east take the lead in restoring order to Syria if Mr Al-Assad leaves. [Re his statements about not trusting the west].

3/12/2012 - PAUL ARMSTRONG - TO SYRIAN PRESIDENT BASHAR AL-ASSAD

3/12/2012

TO SYRIAN PRESIDENT BASHAR AL-ASSAD

Dear Ambassador,

Please can you pass the following on to your President Bashar Al-Assad.

Dear Mr President,

You are saying no and you refuse to listen to the west. But who will you listen to? Admit for a minute you could be wrong. Look at the devastation; you may actually loose this fight and I am not happy about that result – TOO MUCH BLOODSHED – a destroyed Syria; a huge refugee problem. This already exists right now and it is just getting worse. You CAN say I want my neighbours [middle eastern countries] to take the main part in restoring order to Syria after I retire. Choose someone you trust to take over from you and negotiate peace with all parties; Tell your neighbours the things you would like to see done for your country before you leave. PLEASE!

15/10/2012 PAUL ARMSTRONG - TO SYRIAN PRESIDENT BASHAR AL-ASSAD

15/10/2012
TO SYRIAN PRESIDENT BASHAR AL-ASSAD

Dear Sir / Madam,

Please can you pass the following on to President Bashar Al-Assad.

Dear Mr President,

This fighting is not going to end – you both are leaving a trail of destruction in your country and the people are suffering. Your security is not threatened so you feel you can fight on but the Free Syrian Army are thinking the same thing "Our security is not threatened so we can fight on". Eventually people are going to get so sick that you are going to have to talk and I don't want it to take that long. I don't think you can stay on – there is an afterwards; after the fighting; after the bloodshed; and change is going to be expected then – we cannot go back. The free Syrian Army cannot go into power either – there has to be elections; democracy; There has to be a handover of power; there has to be international peacekeepers to keep the peace. There is a lot of work to be done. What can you give? You can give the one thing no one else can give PEACE – you can talk to the international community and say before I go I want this, this and this done when I leave – I want my country looked after. The future will not change on this : fighting will drag out unending - it will not end if you do not retire. Hand over power to someone you trust – an interim administrator to negotiate a peaceful resolution – an intermediary.

18/09/2012 PAUL ARMSTRONG - TO SYRIAN PRESIDENT BASHAR AL ASSAD

18/09/2012
TO SYRIAN PRESIDENT BASHAR AL-ASSAD

Dear Mr Ambassador,

Please can you pass the following on to President Bashar Al-Assad.

 Dear President Bashar,

Violence has to end on all sides. There must be reforms. A significant gesture is needed to start things. The repression must end. This is not just your country it is also the region and the world. There will be more bloodshed more suffering if you do not talk – I hope real talks with all sides can begin soon. i would talk to Mr Brahimi ask him to coordinate talks between yourself and your neighbours on one hand and between the Free Syrian army and yourself on the other. You have to say you are willing to step down if that is the only way there is going to be peace; if that is the only way. I would trust Mr Brahimi – he is a capable negotiator. He is right to focus on the suffering – we all need to focus on that – end that – which means there has to be peace. Mr Brahimi does not have a set agenda he is not out to force you to resign – That should only happen "if that is the only way for peace" – can you accept that?

13/09/2012 PAUL ARMSTRONG - TO SYRIAN ENVOY LAKHDAR BRAHIMI - CEASEFIRE IDEAS

13/09/2012
TO SYRIAN ENVOY LAKHDAR BRAHIMI

Dear Sir / Madam,
Please can you pass the following on to Mr Lakhdar Brahimi. Most of this email contains ideas for negotiating a ceasefire. Thank You.
Dear Mr Brahimi,
I would advise that you get lots of different people all talking to the Free Syrian Army all trying to persuade them to call a complete cessation of violence you can use this for other groups that are reluctant to join the negotiations. Below I enclose a series of ideas for negotiating a ceasefire. I hope they help.
God Bless / Allah Bless You

- Acknowledge wrongs have been committed [to the insurgent group]
- [to insurgent group] Talk to the people you claim to represent – ask them for their opinions – should you negotiate
- Point out to them all terrorist movements move from violence to peace eventually
- Say to them there is a lot of work to be done – even after a ceasefire and peace
- Tell them - If you turn to peace – you can be a lobby movement for your cause – you will probably get more support – model yourself on other peaceful Islamic movements
- Point out to them – now is the best time in history to negotiate
- Ask them what progress they have achieved with violence – not a lot
- Tell them submit your ideas to the public at large
- Tell them you want more members – you are going to have to choose the path of peace
- Tell them you are going to have to talk to other groups – DIALOGUE
- Acknowledge the wrongs that have been committed [to the insurgent group]

I know that you have some just grievances; we have committed wrongs. People have been hurt. But now we want peace. Will you talk to us. The reason you started fighting was because you perceived injustices and wanted to protest against them. Now I am telling you – you can end those injustices and achieve a just peace by talking to us.

- [to insurgent group] Talk to the people you claim to represent – ask them for their opinions – should you negotiate

  Talk to those you represent ask them what they think of the situation. Ask the people on the ground from your community do you want us to negotiate – do you want us to continue fighting. Are you tired of the suffering. Do you trust us to come up with a just settlement for you

- Point out to them all terrorist movements move from violence to peace eventually

  I wish to point out to you – History does repeat itself – all terrorist movements eventually move from fighting to pursuing peace. In the end you too will choose peace it is just a matter of when. Time and again terrorists have realised that there actions stand to succeed more if they turn from violence to peace. Yes violence gave them a voice – but it will not gain them an agreement for that they need to pursue peace.

- Say to them there is a lot of work to be done – even after a ceasefire and peace

  Even when you do choose peace – there is still a lot of work to be done. We need to rebuild this country – heal the wounds of hatred and grief. We need to reintegrate former fighters into peaceful activities. You are a part of this future.

- Tell them - If you turn to peace – you can be a lobby movement for your cause – you will probably get more support – model yourself on other peaceful Islamic movements

  If you turn to peace – you can enter politics – you will be able to talk to the media freely – you will be listened to by a greater audience. You will be heard. You will achieve progress. Please model yourself on other Islamic movements such as the Muslim brotherhood in Egypt. Who knows you may even end up in a coalition government some day.

- Point out to them – now is the best time in history to negotiate

  Now is the best time to negotiate – People are tired of the violence on all sides. There are elements of people ready to listen and negotiate on all sides –politicians have become pragmatic – they know they have to talk to you – that the fighting is only leading to a stalemate. This was not so in the past.

- Ask them what progress they have achieved with violence – not a lot

  What progress have you made using violence – Not a lot. You have been fighting for several years now. All I see is a war of attrition with neither side able to defeat the other completely. If you do not try and take the peace option what does the future hold for you - only continued strife and suffering for everyone.

- Tell them submit your ideas to the public at large

  If you choose peace – you will be given the opportunity to submit your ideas to the public at large. You will be addressing more people than you ever have before and what's more the press will not be reporting you in a hostile way instead in an open business like way. But you must choose peace for this to happen.

- Tell them - you want more members – you are going to have to choose the path of peace
  You are not a large organisation – at least not directly speaking and the people are getting tired of violence – that's where the majority of people lie. If you wish to become a bigger organisation and have a real voice – if you wish to recruit more members you are going to have to choose the path of peace.

- Tell them - you are going to have to talk to other groups – DIALOGUE
  You cannot act in isolation forever – you need to broaden your base; you want other people to listen to you – you are going to have to talk to other groups – This means dialogue – To come out of this isolation you must choose peace.

12/09/2012 PAUL ARMSTRONG - TO SYRIAN ENVOY LAKHDAR BRAHIMI - SOME PEACE IDEAS + LETTER TO FREE SYRIAN ARMY

12/09/2012
TO SYRIAN ENVOY LAKHDAR BRAHIMI

Dear Sir / Madam,
Please can you pass the following on to Mr Lakhdar Brahimi as I know he has worked for you. If you are not going to pass these ideas AND letter on to him please tell me. Thank you.
   Dear Mr Brahimi,
I enclose a letter which you could address to the Free Syrian Army. I hope they are included in the talks and that they commit to peace. I also enclose some ideas on peace.
Allah Bless You / God Bless You
   TO FREE SYRIAN ARMY
You are going to have to nominate someone to talk for you. The violence is not going to end if you don't. I would put my trust in Lakhdar Brahimi he is a pretty capable negotiator – he has brought peace before. You are going to have to work with others anyway no matter the outcome – that is an important realisation. Eventually there is going to have to be round table talks on the future of Syria – THIS IS A DEFINITE. Re The Syrian leader it does not look like you are going to get rid of him in one go [In armed conflict I think his side is slightly stronger than you] – Lets see what you can come up with in negotiations. Again Lakhdar Brahimi is pretty capable. Ask for permission to nominate someone – someone you trust to represent you in talks [as long as Lakhdar accepts your nominee it should be okay]. Now this would be a good concession to gain at the start of talks : the concession of allowing your side to be represented. You are going to have to hold peace for the talks.

- Distribution of resources

- Don't concentrate all power in the hands of the president – actors more likely to participate if power is shared
- Attackers can nominate someone to talk for them – tell them either you talk or the violence will not end
- Establish the parameters of the talks at the start
- Give your own helpful commentary on what each side tells you to the other side
- Civilian control of the police
- A significant gesture from both sides at the beginning of negotiations
- A civil society secretariat that can question government policy and even take the government to the constitutional court
- Regions can have some influence over local education
- Minority vetoes on certain issues
- Hold a national conference - international observers present at these talks would add influence for results of conference to be implemented
- Media rights for indigenous peoples
- A state language and indigenous languages recognised

TO PRESIDENT ASSAD - PAUL ARMSTRONG

6/08/2012

TO SYRIAN PRESIDENT BASHAR AL ASSAD

Dear Sir / Madam,

Please can you let President Assad read this letter.

 Dear Mr Assad,

Listen; This war is not going to end any time soon AND there is going to be alot more bloodshed ALOT. I am not happy about this and I really don't think you like having to kill so many people. I don't think you want to have to do this. Even if you win what is the result. What are the Free Syrian Army trying to achieve - a democracy - a real democracy. A lot of people have come together on this side from all spectrums even from within your own army. A lot of people want change. It is difficult to say I resign - the first step is the hardest - You don't have to make any public statements just retire - let someone else take control - someone you accept. And let the person you hand over power to - talk to the Free Syrian Army - So that no more Men Women and Children die. You have to focus on your family - a private life in a new country that agrees to offer

you a place - a home.
P.S.
Your Life Is Not Over!

PEACE IN SYRIA - PAUL ARMSTRONG

25/07/2012

TO SYRIAN PRESIDENT - BASHAR AL ASSAD

Dear Sir / Madam,

Please, please can you let President Bashar Al Assad read this.

Dear Mr Assad,

I see you are unpopular. The violence is not going to end. You have two options – one is going to be bloody whatever the outcome – I know; I know; I know you don't want to leave – I want peace for Syria and it is looking like you are going to have to leave. Listen I would say no more bloodshed; The difficult part is the first few steps announcing your resignation. Now I don't want you going to prison AND you are not happy right now. What is the future? It is looking like a new government; it is looking like a third party country accepts you – that you live in peace with your family. When you make this decision – you are saying I am not going to cling to power at all costs; I accept that politicians and leaders change; I accept that I have to choose this or there will not be peace; I accept UN sanctions will not end unless I do this. What will happen if you go? Syria will need help – I know this too – but the UN and the international community will help the country – they are not going to let Syria go backwards.

P.S

Your Life Is Not Over!

#2 PAUL ARMSTRONG - TO AMBASSADOR IMAD MOUSTAPHA

28/11/2011

TO SYRIAN PRESIDENT - BASHAR AL ASSAD

Dear Ambassador,

Can you pass the following on to your President Bashar Al-Assad.

Dear Mr. Assad,

I want you to concede issues. I want you to realise how serious this is. The Arab league does not want to replace you. You are being isolated right now because you refuse to listen to your people – that is how the world sees it. I will be frank here the world sees you as some kind of self-appointed leader who will not listen to democracy. How do you intend to respond to these claims? I would talk to the opposition – now obviously you are the one who will be making the concessions – they have nothing to give you. Is it right to do this? Democracy is good, freedom of speech is good, freedom to protest is good – if you are preventing these things then that is not good. I am not trying to replace you as leader of your country that is for your people in elections to freely decide. Listen – take a moment – ignore the voices outside of your country and ask yourself how am I going to solve this problem peacefully without harm to the people. You could use a minister of your government to talk to the protestors. Are you prepared for this?... There Will Be Change!

The Key Words Here Are – There Will Be Change!

EMPLOYMENT IDEAS

Purpose : Provide a list of employment generation ideas for the Muslim world and for countries recovering from conflict. Key ideas are in bold text.

- Renaming sports stadiums to company's brand-name. E.g. the Aviva rugby stadium in Ireland [Aviva are a private insurance company]
- Advertise more of your culture and heritage in foreign countries - longer lasting advertising
- Turnkey" companies - they act as wholesalers for other companies - provide supply on demand to them
- Another company recommending your product
- Specialise in niche areas such as diagnostics in medicine; sports products; health and beauty products [the latter is a growth area] - Ireland has done this
- Products for the disabled of all kinds - this is a growth area
- Sports teams going public on the stock exchange - E.g. Manchester United have done this
- Language interpreters for hire company - short / long term
- Build museums - natural history / arts / historical artefacts etc.
- Create mobile apps for phones - iphones / android / windows - can charge a small price - make it available in other languages
- Attracting conferences to your country - this would benefit tourism
- Attract world sporting events in niche areas such as hockey, volleyball, basketball, Paralympics / boxing
- Balkan / Arab "city of culture" designated for a particular year

- Waste management companies - dealing with domestic and industrial waste - recycling involved here - people pay by weight of their non-recyclable waste
- Country body provides awards for innovation and science breakthroughs - to businesses / individuals - Highlight the awards on television
- Companies providing assistance to colleges to produce PHD students
- Get a town / city in your country to specialise in creative products - e.g. - jewellery, painting / arts and crafts - Have short-term training courses in a particular skill - not the capital of the country
- Produce software in niche markets banks / small shops / accountancy software
- Internet, media, entertainment, biotechnology, medical devices - these are all areas that venture capitalists are willing to work in
- A business services company
- A business developing accountancy software for their country
- A manager of a company should talk to individuals within the company - for morale purposes
- Find out the business models of other companies - where are their sources
- Peripheral add-ons for other products
- In third level entrepreneurial courses should include training in 1. Knowledge about various industries 2. Knowledge about markets of each industrial sector 3. knowledge of products / technologies
- Develop prototypes of products to advertise to potential customers
- Take on new innovations - pioneers - develop their products further
- Agricultural tools / machines - the third world will be a growth area here - start with low cost products
- Make companies compete on the free market after having protected them initially
- Government sets long term goals for development in industry
- Service guarantees for a set number of years - advertise that
- No-frills airlines - cheap flights would attract more tourists - Ryanair in Ireland is an example of this
- Literacy rates are strongly tied to economic growth
- Support businesses that require large numbers of employees - grants from government to do this

- Fix your exchange rate with other countries - Businesses then can know the cost of doing business internationally. i.e. peg your currency to the Euro or the US Dollar
- Start a business within your own home
- Former leaders / members of local government get involved in entrepreneurship
- Target well-off communities for your business first
- Increase the number of shares of a business at same stock exchange sale price
- Research a history of family businesses as a book - case studies - interview employees on this
- Socialise with prospective customers
- Build fishing boats of different sizes there is room for competition here
- Construction of railways and highways - Ireland followed this idea
- Private shareholding in state-owned enterprises to a degree
- Expand your business to the most industrialised part of the country
- Family businesses ensure your children get a good education
- Set up a second centre of growth in the country
- Getting feedback from relatives / family members / friends about products - ideas for improvement
- Encourage founders of family businesses to pass on control to the next generation as early as possible
- Business visits from companies in the same sector - share knowledge
- Second-generation family members going abroad for their education - widen their horizons
- Have more than one R&D team in the company
- Politicians advising companies
- An R&D company - other companies produce the products - R&D company lives off the royalties
- Graphic design companies for advertising / packaging
- Families of Founders of family businesses grow up in the business - be familiar with all aspects of the business
- Founder's children get employment in other companies in same market area - gain experience there before returning to their parents business

- Do what you want to do in third level education - may give you a different perspective on work when you return to the firm
- State-business partnerships for businesses created - if there is a viable / strategic interest
- Produce third world products - high-protein foods; electricity [solar lighting]; wind-up radios; famine relief goods; affordable irrigation pumps; cheap basic construction materials; basic medical supplies
- Social enterprises are tax free
- Education firms working with UNESCO for books for third world countries
- Ask NGO'S what their needs are - make a business out of their needs
- Venture philanthropy funds for social enterprises
- A social enterprise stock exchange for Europe; MENA countries - governments can get involved in buying shares
- Use biotechnology for the benefit of the third world - more resilient crops - Not like Monsanto with their "suicide seeds"
- A website portal for social enterprises across the Balkans; MENA countries
- Charities supporting SE projects
- Multinational companies sharing patents with SE companies
- Group loans - A group takes out a loan together [unsecured] to start a business - could be family members or a group of friends
- Local currencies similar to the Euro currencies to stimulate consumption within the community - The central bank produces these currencies.
- Social enterprises produce a kit as a guide to other SE companies setting up
- An industrial bank; An agricultural bank
- Building satellites - a state company for this but also serves customers
- An arab space agency - This would generate spin-off companies
- A consumer magazine - rating products like the magazine "Which"
- Must reduce corruption to attract FDI
- Low corporation tax - This worked for Ireland

- Diaspora - remittances to a community rather than an individual - Mexico has done this
- Divide your country into regions with administrations for each investment / foreign investment
- Fast shipping of goods - very efficient customs for imports / exports - reduce costs here
- Make public service more efficient here - eliminate bureaucracy
- Pensions are invested in government - The longer you contribute to a pension - the larger your fund on retirement
- Create similar company laws / tax regimes for business to the foreign country you are trying to attract businesses from
- Target specific countries for investment - such as Germany, Japan, South Korea, UK etc.
- Create international accountancy firms with their main base in your country - Target accountancy firms to your country
- Target expanding markets - India, China
- Sell off state banks - this would make them more competitive
- Manufacturing religious goods for religions in your country / abroad
- Aircraft maintenance is a growth industry
- No fees for third level education
- E-Learning courses / long distance courses with international standards - Improves educational participation
- If others in your country are exporting to another country this makes it easier for you to export to the country
- Target growth areas in other countries - first base to establish a foreign branch of company e.g. Catalonia in Spain and Northern Italy in Italy
- Private colleges also have fees covered by the government
- International financial services companies setting up in your country - low taxes
- Affordable baby-sitting facilities to allow both parents to work
- Enter foreign markets as soon as possible
- Set up religious shops around mosques, churches
- Set up tourist centres along the coast such as Ibiza island in Spain

- Internship for students to partnered colleges in other countries - an exchange for both sides
- Train the trainers for improved quality of education in third level colleges via "education firms"
- Restaurants near churches / Mosques / schools
- Small companies who sell to large companies - large companies get a share in others business
- Set up a wholesaler business in another country for products made in home country
- Can purchase a passport if you invest 1 million in an indigenous company
- If your company has profits invest in shares in other companies<
- Hire people with English language skills - English is the international language of business
- Establish R&D centres in other countries will benefit the home company as well as the host country
- Every team member in the company can make suggestions for new ideas; improvements to products
- A printing press that serves more than one media outlet
- Mini-businesses within schools - for children to gain an experience in Entrepreneurship
- Embassies setting up contacts for home businesses
- Use advertising on "Facebook", "Linked In" - these are growth industries
- Producing educational materials for schools - cheaper books - Recruit the best teachers to draw up the curriculum
- University professors producing educational materials for third level colleges across Arab region
- Upmarket goods for tourist industry - clothes, food etc.
- Pedestrianise inner city shopping areas for shopping for tourists
- Import second hand cars - cheaper for people to buy
- Food ingredients for food products is a growth industry

- Telephone cards - This company buys phone call costs in bulk from telecoms - Families can purchase them and contact their immigrant relatives - a growth market here
- Advertise that a certain percentage of the price of goods goes to a charity
- Government grants to become carbon-neutral
- Green entrepreneurship college courses
- Green shops - environmentally friendly / carbon neutral / fair trade / respecting forests e.g. Forest Stewardship council
- Research into dealing with sewage - a group of universities take this on
- Phase out incandescent lighting / plastic bags
- Foreign MNC's must follow environmental laws of home country
- Start as a charity business - later develop commercially
- Talk about the history of your company on your company website
- Go public on other stock exchanges early on
- Advertising on mobile phones is a growth market
- Have notable CEO's on your board - good for marketing
- Have a local phone number for each country - redirect to your company
- A memorable phone number for your business
- Advertise on Facebook
- Have videos on your website - introducing your company and its products
- Purchase equipment for your business from companies that are closing down
- Venture companies doing tours with your company in other countries / own country
- Importing second-hand computers - Universities frequently upgrade their computers - So a good market here
- Diagnostics in the health sciences is a growth industry
- A nation-wide open wi-fi network - pay at home can be used anywhere in the country
- Companies should have more than one business site in the country - Different aspects of the business in different parts of the country
- Outsource production within a country as much as possible
- Create value brands for supermarkets

- Allow e-procurement - advertise in different countries - quicker purchasing and problem solving responses
- Hazardous waste companies
- Set up recycling companies to take materials from other countries
- Railway links with ports for faster transport of goods to different countries linked by rails
- Associate transport companies with ports
- Build ports along maritime corridors; example for Egypt near the Suez canal
- Speed up customs clearances - entering / leaving the country
- Online reviews of products by customers
- Keep pension investments within the country
- Products for the elderly - Europe has an ageing population - so this is a growth market - Interview elderly people about their needs
- Spare parts company - all leading brands - in electrical / car parts
- A business developing water treatment plants - Make law towns / cities over a certain size must have full water treatment facilities
- Safety equipment for construction industry is a growth area for jobs
- Citing patents in journals - explaining what the patents mean
- Hotel federations sponsor festivals
- Separate out waste collection - food waste / recyclable waste / clothing / glass / other waste
- Temporary workers must be made permanent after six months
- A "Made In Egypt" "Made In Greece" logo on your products
- Buy future shares in a company agree to pay on a certain date if the price of the shares goes up you can sell them immediately and make a profit
- Renting products
- Pairing products with shops - we only sell at such a shop company - receive a bonus for doing this
- Making donations to charity - have charities advertise your companies for this
- Getting a fair trade products logo
- Services for free initially / demo versions of products
- Discount vouchers / chances to win prizes if they buy your products
- Check out what your competition is doing and copy or improve on it

- Businesses must register themselves to pay taxes
- Keep your social welfare payments for a number of years after starting a business
- Market yourself as a regional port e.g. Egypt for north Africa and the Middle East or Greece for the south-east Europe - Businesses tend to develop around major ports
- Agricultural colleges
- Develop a product in a market that already has similar products - find a niche in it.
- Give your products on a rental basis
- Get large businesses to market your products - they get a percentage of the profits
- Use Google add words to market your products over the internet
- Mini-markets - try your products at universities / colleges / schools first
  Start-ups merge your business with another start-up in the same field
- Entrepreneurship as a subject in secondary school
- Ask yourself - "would I buy this product"
- Have a shopping television channel where demonstrations are provided. This can be done on a pan-Balkan pan-Arab basis. Choose locally / regionally produced products to advertise first
- Making partnerships - one person provides the financing [a majority proportion] and another runs the business - Both share in the profits
- Alternative perks to keep your employees - free lunches / child care services
- Business / government forms online to eliminate corruption
- Business fairs for young students - influence their life choices
- Networks of scientists working on a project - results shared by all involved for setting up business ventures [more likely to happen this way]
- Start with supporting businesses that have low production costs and gradually advance the industry
- Forming social networks :- professional, leisure, religion, political and voluntary organisations - Get references from them to secure money from banks
- Renting equipment for startup companies - a fraction of the original cost on yearly / monthly basis. Especially from universities

- First-Choice : companies going into universities and offering jobs to students who will soon finish college
- A government retirement fund for academics / scientists to keep them in the country
- Charities asking and funding companies to do research in health sciences
- A science magazine for Arab / Balkan region - similar to Nature magazine in the US
- The higher the level of democracy in a country the more FDI you will receive
- A government reward scheme for researchers who come up with new employable ideas
- Governments to match venture capitalist funds 1 to 1
- Register your business in the local domain name of a country on internet search engines | Have your own website in other languages
- A business court with implementing powers for local and multinational companies
- Link universities with primary / secondary schools
- Producing products for ethnic Diaspora especially in the food market - Encourage disapora to set up companies to import these products from home
- Companies provide technology licenses to other countries companies on a franchise business. A good example would be in the pharmaceutical area - locally produced international brands [It has been done in Ireland]
- In-firm promotions to encourage workers to stay in the company especially exemplary ones
- Engineers make better managers as can be seen from the case in Germany
- A company magazine for employees
- Get ideas from life experiences to form new companies
- Publish your contributions to society / social projects - creates an indispensable positive brand image in customers minds
- College courses for green entrepreneurship
- Green laws such as WEEE [Waste Electrical and Electronic Equipment]
- Encourage students to pursue courses in education where you have targeted industry

- Set up smaller companies during a downturn in economy when large businesses close. For example Microsoft, Nokia, Google and Samsung electronics all were born during these downturns. Less obstacles to compete against
- Policy laws that force companies to adopt certain strategies / investments such as in the greening of their business to environmentally sound practices
- Focusing industries around airports / seaports
- Cross-border broadband networks for Arab region / Balkans
- Companies providing referrals / references of other companies they have been involved with Market places for specific product types on the internet and also physical markets for things such as agricultural products, media, ICT, electronic
- Develop carbon trading industries - attract investment here
- Develop similar networks to Facebook for Arab / Balkan region
- You need to have successful entrepreneurs recruited to represent your economy in other countries for attracting inward investment / developing links between national and foreign companies
- Attract industry leading companies Microsoft / Samsung etc. - provide incentives for this - They can then act as anchor companies to attract other companies in the same field
- Draw up national development plans with civil society, educational institutions and business for next 10 years
- Produce cheap mobile phones - China produces mobile phones as cheap as $13
- Make it law that leading software companies must make their coding available to budding entrepreneurs
- Advanced education for bright students - university training
- A platform for large companies to advertise their requirements over the internet to prospective local businesses
- Translation services provided by government.

- Target companies that have a large number of suppliers such as General Electric
- Industries providing academic skills training with their companies in colleges
- Free land grants for industry
- Introduce competition in the telecommunications sector
- Language training in a particular language should be a part of every college course
- Local language translation of international products [instructions] software applications etc
- NGO's involved in skills training
- Develop cooperatives for agriculture - consolidate them into a few large companies - In the long run this will generate more jobs - Ireland did this
- Peer-to-peer training from successful entrepreneurs
- Companies subsidising prospective students in college who will then work in their companies
- Unemployed graduates given training in a similar field [short top-up courses]
- Establishing a formal Diaspora network - to work on building links between home industries and foreign companies. Supporting by advertising brands abroad
- Hire skilled people on contract
- Government subsidies for users NOT producers of industry - this will sustain demand in early stages of company development
- Link up with other successful zones in other countries
- Advertise your business in the media eg. newspapers
- Specialise in a new particular industry in your country
- Micro projects in schools - set up an imaginary business - hold a competition on this across the country
- Develop culture in your cities :- arts, festivals, exhibitions, sports - fund such
- activities - cultural activities in a city will attract businesses
- Government provide financing for companies to cooperate with each other

- Regional international airports to attract businesses
- A database of industries in your country available to foreign countries / foreign businesses
- Advertise your list of clients - especially if they are big companies
- Partnering with local companies in foreign market if you want to enter that market
- Ask clients to provide recommendations / references
- Try to be the biggest in your market make that your goal
- One of the best ways to gain experience about what it is like to set up a startup is to join an existing startup first
- When pitching for investors bring along other members of your team to pitch there for you too at the meeting
- Your business commenting in the media :- local and national on business issues to get your name out. Try in foreign makets you intend entering or developing
- Company produce a magazine - send to prospective customers/businesses regularly. Could include facts about your country/culture; Profiles of employees who work for you; Prizes eg. a free trip to your country
- Cross cultural training programs :- introduce foreign businessmen/businesswomen to these programs for free - invite them to your country for this
- Meet the people/companies your wholesaler/distributor is working with personally
- Host business meetings of prospective customers at embassies
- Create bi-national business associations eg. Greece-America society to promote trade both ways | provide a social forum for people with common interests
- Buy a foreign company from another country and then get it to set up base in your country
- Two companies entering into joint ventures where the two create a third company – they share in the profits of the company
- Buy a small company in another country [in the same area of production as yourself] - then amalgamate it into your own business - you now have access to a new established market base
- Laws in a country that demand access to coding of software products so indigenous companies can create their own complimentary software
- Locate trade professionals in foreign embassies to help local industry export there / hire out highly experienced local officials to assist at the embassy
- Businesses doing demonstrations of their products/services to public/particular company/companies

- Make it easy for business people to enter your country and stay there Hire mature people in industry as business advisors in government agencies to help new startups
- Foreign embassies keeping track of buyers for home country
- Know your customers [businesses] [plus for new businesses / customers] - the more you know about the company - its products and its position in the marketplace the better you appear to them
- Encourage your employees to spend a certain amount of their time on planning in other areas of the business
- Develop a "sample" contract to buyers initially :- companies more willing to try your product out in home and export markets
- Localized translation service companies for international software products
- Several universities collaborating on a project
- Governments tender for a cluster of industries to providee services to SMEs : provide cheaper services and standardization
- Set up an Education Special Zone - that attracts worldclass educational institutes from abroad to create a learning hub in your country
- Free trials of your product
- Create your own tools for your business and then market them for sale
- People can visit your company's site location : customers / potential business partners. They can interview lead employees
- Advertise your business / product on another companies DIFFERENT product. eg. A sticker on bananas
- Every so often businesses provide a reward to regular customers for their loyalty
- Always ask for something you want even if you think you cannot get it
- Hire employees on a trial basis first before signing a full contract
- Crowdfunding : On the internet an entrepreneur makes a business proposal. People make pledges for the project - if enough money is raised the project goes ahead. Pledgers recieve a share in the business for their financial contribution
- Managers should set ambitious targets for profits
- Managers being able to speak foreign languages is an advantage for spreading your market worldwide

- Go international [set up business branches in other countries] early on in your business
- Companies bringing politicians / notable / famous people to another country to meet with other trade representatives / companies on a social basis
- Don't employ salespeople - get those who are responsible for a project [managers] to market it / negotiate with customers
- Famous people praising / using a product in their relevant field eg. cyclists using carbon wheels from a company that produces them
- Smaller business units [separate] are closer to customers
- Provide the services along with the business eg. Bauer : It not only manufactures special drilling equipment, but also provides the corresponding drilling services
- Cover the entire value chain for your product eg. Neumann Group : Neumann manages coffee plantations, treats the green coffee, takes care of export and import logistics, and supplies the roasting houses in target markets
- All business regulations should be available in one booklet and simplified as much as possible and in plain language
- Business feedback to government - This is how each business regulation is affecting us
- Reducing government business administrative costs will increase GDP
- Business associations encouraging their members to register their business officially
- For marketing your products it is good to have a slogan like Nike: "Just do it" or Intel : "Intel Inside"
- Invest more in the arts – film-making / cinema / documentaries / TV production / radio / Satellite / theatre – A tax break for these industries [no taxes]
- A pan-arab meeting place for enterprises on the internet – a forum – where entrepreneurs can develop contacts / exchange experiences / exchange ideas
- Set up a panel to review / endorse new products / services of start-up firms. A star-rating [do not have to publish results for a firm]

- Tap into unemployed previous entrepreneurs – encourage them to start again [cancel their previous debts if they have a new viable business proposal]
- You need to invest in telecommunications – phone / internet / mobile phone infrastructure
- Environmental technologies is going to be a growth area in the future – water management / recycling / biofuels / biomass / environmental waste treatment. This is an industry worth investing in.
- Government support/business centres should be located where the businesses are for easy access
- Form cooperatives – in industries start-ups / agriculture – allows access to more financing / more purchasing power / ability to improve their businesses more easily
- Businesses working together with a state research body – results of research are made available to all participating firm
- If firms are clustered together / or in industrial parks they are more likely to receive venture finance
- An agency makes companies aware of new technologies / new ways of doing things – provide financing for companies to upgrade [a technology fund] – need this agency to be familiar with industries in other countries to do this
- Need to promote entrepreneurship in the media and in schools
- Venture capitalists should be provided with access to information – how the business is run and how it intends to run / monitor the progress of the firm over time
- Companies are more likely to form alliances if they are located together in industrial parks
- Firms will locate to where there is venture capital available locally
- Encourage location of foreign firms to your country that are in the same industrial sector as a main indigenous industry [an industry you want to develop further] – could stimulate the economy | force local industry to improve | +knowledge spillovers
- State companies supporting individuals in setting up their own companies [with finance / logistics / marketing] – individuals develop product for proposal – They are given a reward if successful
- Customers partnering with a spin-off to form a new company
- Encourage people to return home and set up a business from the west etc.

- Business fairs – companies hold a stall where you display info on your company and its services | Hold business fairs in other countries too
- Portfolio companies – have a list of companies and their products for you to choose from in each industry sector
- Brokers – You say you are looking for a particular product or service and the broker links you to a company
- Entrepreneurial managers within a company supporting / fostering new businesses
- Governments asking firms to do research for them to develop technologies [outside of military area!] and provide funding for this. Individual state departments doing this. Companies can keep rights to products developed.
- Host conventions in other countries for industry – advertise – the services / grants / supports your country provides to industry [especially target particular industrial sectors such as electronics / engineering / biotechnology / teleservices]
- Conferences in developing particular industries – hosted by national government foundations such as National Science Foundation / National Agricultural Foundation / National Tourism Foundation – for industry
- Get lots of experience in different jobs before you choose to become an entrepreneur
- Adult education centres
- You need someone to review your business every so often – compare it with the competition [home/abroad] / latest technology / costs in the firm – someone from outside an expert
- Low tax zones/areas where businesses can locate
- Government supplements wages of employees for new firms in their first few years [where wages are low] – firms need to be a certain size to be competitive
- A business telephone directory with addresses and adverts containing business details such as products offered by companies as well as products being developed
- Develop regions with historical industries – invest in these regions/modernise them
- Have companies specifically designed to sell other companies products
- You need a stable exchange rate to grow economy – peg your currency to the dollar
- Outsourcing of processes from existing firms [specialization]

- Close interaction with clients – share your ideas with them/what you are developing/give clients access to your R&D ask for their feedback/inputs | What are your competitors saying to them
- A government minister for enterprise and employment
- Raise the profile of entrepreneurs in the media – to make entrepreneurship more culturally acceptable
- A degree course in entrepreneurship – businesses that have graduates from this kind of course have higher growth rates
- Allow firms to employ people without fixed long-term contracts – if it is difficult to fire people – small businesses will be reluctant to hire people in the first place due to the expenses involved if they later have to fire an employee – "flexible labour laws". This will lead to a stronger economy.
- One office in government to deal with entrepreneurs – a single entry point for entrepreneurs dealing with all matters – regulation, registration, taxes etc.
- Professional short training courses for entrepreneurs to improve their business skills – provided by government agency – skills to start and develop a business / training in managing a company and in exports and sales
- Each government department has its own entrepreneurship budget – ministry of finance / ministry of agriculture / ministry of health etc. – develop industries relevant to their area of expertise
- Assistance in marketing to the right people – industries/communities/retail that need your product
- Talk to people you know [family/friends/relatives] who have started their own business get their advice/help in starting your own business
- Government/State research bodies for industry such as in biotechnology/computers/chemical/electronics – locate them in industry clusters or next to universities – learn how to do this from other countries
- Colleges helping students find a job
- Pay people to set up a business in your country
- Job placement for students during college years for six months in third year of a four year degree course [job in area relative to course you are doing]

- Contract out government functions to private sector
- Negotiate access to western markets for products [get them to remove trade barriers etc.] in return for cheaper oil [you need to diversify your industrial base away from oil]
- Small business association – provides advice, lobby group, a business fund to act as a surety against bank loans, hiring the right people
- Government targeting a certain amount of contracts to small businesses
- Share patent rights/intellectual rights with other Arab countries
- No taxes for businesses for the first three years of businesses
- Break up industrial monopolies [state monopoly industries] this will lead to greater economic growth
- University staff/professors can work part-time in companies being developed [spin-offs from university] | Can take a sabbatical from university for up to two years to work in business spin-off [without loosing university job and continuing to receive 50% of university wages during this time]
- Provide ground-space [free-rent] for start-up companies [several start-up companies in the one building]
- Reduce costs of bankruptcy to the entrepreneur state act as a guarantor for a large part of any debts that may be incurred]
- Copy foreign firms located in your country [in industrial zones] – take advantage of knowledge spill-over – access to workers from those firms [countries in the Asian-Pacific rim such as South Korea have done this]
- Emigrants who have become entrepreneurs in foreign countries encouraged to come home and set up similar business – provide incentives for them to do this
- A bank that does small business loans [like the Grameen bank in Bangladesh]
- Government business grants – for setting up a business in areas where you want to promote industry growth [including for foreign industries]
- If you have a patent/prototype you are more likely to receive venture capital / investments
- Financial incentives for university scientists to make their research commercially viable
- Break up a large company into individual sectoral industries – makes them more profitable / competiitive

- Help firms that are in debt – get someone from outside to do a review of the business | get new customers | relocate to a new base | reschedule debts | look for new sources of suppliers
- Firms branch out to a bigger market / bigger city in your country
- Encourage people to invest in a business – will be given money back gradually when company goes public
- If you are a big investor you can get a position on the board of management
- Sell your business to others – stay on as managers of the company
- Hand the running of the business over to professionals while you maintain ownership of the company
- Buyer telling seller what they are looking for in a product even passing specific knowledge to them to assist in the development of new product
- Allow people to change jobs easily [in technology sectors] increases knowledge pool in society / across industries – could lead to more start-up industries
- Internal units within established companies with autonomy to do their own research / innovation
- A public directory of investors – angel investors [individuals] / venture capitalists – sorted by category of industry they are interested in and where they are located
- Advertise your business proposal online [internet at a website [designed for this job]] for investors to search through
- Universities / technical colleges / private colleges in a region specialise in a certain technology / industry – [to help develop clusters of industry in a region / city]
- Industry provides colleges with latest research facilities / equipment – which would enable colleges to do more research for industries in return
- Encourage people to use the internet – get their business on the internet – [build more internet cafes – lots of them]
- Provide people with bank accounts with a bank card that can be used online [a debit card [cash already in account]] – this will result in more spending on Arab internet based businesses.
- If someone has previous business/entrepreneurial experience I would be more likely to support him re: grants/bank loan

- Start up a business if you loose your job in the same area as you worked in
- Skills training – you get paid while doing these courses – set up by the government in key industry areas – you do not need any qualifications to apply for one of these courses
- Hire 3rd level students from around the world to do research for your company – so you can produce a new product
- Buy a business and invest money in it – expand it – other companies/wealthy people
- Be willing to support a person in starting another business if their previous business has failed
- Turn something you really like doing / hobby into a business
- Business centres in each city – a place where business people can go to get contacts of other businesses – advertise their own businesses; get information on financial aids grants available to them; get access to mentors; meet other business people there; establish social networks there; provide secretarial services; meet banks there; store CV's of people seeking employment;
- Don't change the interest rate on a bank loan for businesses permanently
- Sharing your job with someone else – an apprenticeship in important jobs – managerial / computers / chemical – job experience – so they can set up their own business [state owned companies could do this] – give them real experience in industries where there is job growth potential
- A pan-Arab stock market for innovative companies – to raise money [venture capitalists]
- Attract R&D investment from foreign companies to your country to universities as a way of anchoring companies in your country – they could set up a new branch company here
- A skills firm / body – provides skilled advisers in an industry to assist a company in developing a new product / service
- Get external technicians from other companies [suppliers] to work in your company [in your factory] temporarily to assist in the development

of new products – this company can expect to receive help back in return if it needs it

- Government tender foreign firms to implement a big project on condition they set up a company within the country to service the industry for domestic markets and for exports from this country
- Universities must be involved in the local community
- Franchise stores [in other countries] to sell the products of a company / group of companies from your country e.g. like Benetton and Diesel
- Tender companies to produce a product/service where it is needed in your country/where there is a demand. You can ask foreign companies already established in your country to manufacture the extra product in your country. Tell companies if you want to sell something in our country you must produce it in our country. Ask people to set up a business in your country.
- Big businesses that are inefficient – set up small companies to fill in the niches – they will be more competitive | be more profitable | cheaper | and in the long run create more jobs as they move into more markets. Some people say "life costs too much these days" – private companies to replace state run enterprises/services [niches at the start] will leave the state with more money to use as it chooses
- New training for employees/managers related to the work they do
- Advertise your skills base [educated youth] to companies in other countries for inward investment – you are going to have to work with 3rd level colleges to specialise in certain areas at the start
- If a new/small business has been in existence for more than four years – that is a good indicator that it is a solid business – invest in these kinds of businesses for the most job creating potential
- Colleges publish your research locally in business journals so entrepreneurs can take up the research and turn it into a business / more than one company will probably do this
- Establish yourself as a niche business within an industry e.g. window wipers for cars; zips for clothes; etc.
- Develop industries in new international growth areas – biotechnology/environmental/computer software

- purchase the rights to produce old products from companies – old computers / mobile phones / cars
- Get local companies to purchase international patents – there is a market there of unused patents : governments assist companies in doing this
- Set up an industrial development body with branch offices in highly progressive regions of other countries such as Silicon valley/ Ruhr valley to market businesses from your country and attract businesses from these regions to your country
- Work as a team with others to set up a business [businesses where teams lead are usually more successful than individual start-ups]
- If you think a business is a viable idea – fund them even if they are making losses for a few years
- Invest in low-capital businesses – they start up quicker and become profitable quicker
- If you have a natural resource – invite businesses into your country to create derived industries there – livestock exporting transformed into a meat production industry by incoming industries | oil exporting transformed into oil products/plastics/clothes etc. by incoming industries
- When a company sends out a bill – include promotional material on other services provided by the company of that others offer – include discounts . vouchers
- Tell people what went wrong in your business – learn from the mistakes of others
- Tell students in college what you [business] are looking for in a recruit while they are in college
- Recruit experts from abroad to set up a business in your country
- Encourage people in management / experienced positions to branch out and set up their own business
- Business owner – leave a business once it is established firmly and set up a new one : – government provide incentives for owners to do this
- Business assisting new businesses : mentoring / selling their product for a set number of years after which the become independent [state companies could do this in some countries on a regional basis where there is limited private industry]
- Teaching students in school about procedures involved in setting up a business – make it part of the educational system
- People can choose how part of their taxes are invested : in community / funding business creation / social projects. They can choose to pay extra

for special projects : re business creation they can invest their money and receive a portion of profits made by businesses in their region on an amalgamated basis each year – like a pension. They must choose to invest in something!

- Every time a firm reaches a milestone they get more investment from the state – when they hire more than ten employees / when they make their first operating profit / when they expand their business into a second location / when they expand their sales outside the city |region |country. – Reward Them!
- Let employees buyout a company if it is failing – including the product rights – governments providing financing for this
- An auction to sell off failed businesses
- Companies working with universities to develop/research new products / Research students spending time working for companies
- A company that buys other failing companies and restores them to profit
- Get companies to work together on developing a product with/without university assistance
- If you have an idea – source it out to a company for them to produce it
- Encourage multinationals to source materials locally / work with local partners
- produce a product that has been simplified – more relevant to what customers want
- manufacture a product for another company for them to sell
- If you come from a foreign country and set up a business in a country you can gain citizenship in that country
- forming an alliance with an established firm
- Develop trade links with diaspora business people in other countries
- Invite people to come to your country and visit a business
- Clustering of similar businesses will attract international businesses
- Invest in clusters – where people know someone who is an entrepreneur they are more likely to set up their own business
- Subcontracting is important – find out what a company needs
- A body marketing several companies products
- Hometown unions / religious associations for informal sector – provide access to finance / business contacts

- Informal sector businesses register through hometown unions – state collects taxes indirectly through associations
- Businesses provide concessions to other hometown union members – an incentive to join the association
- Wherever you come from – going back to your community to invest there once a year
- Small and medium sized businesses given a voice in parliament
- Government providing / getting companies to do research for them and then they develop that into a business
- Sector knowledge – build information packs for entrepreneurs
- If you have a business you can get a free consultation on improving your business
- The cost of starting a business must be cheap – this is what decides on whether a person will start up a business – provide people with free secretarial / accounting / marketing [someone to market your product] / assistance with R&D / and pay for prototypes. A body set up to do these things
- Local businesses hold a fair in their town
- An Arab R&D fund
- A business magazine highlighting entrepreneurs / new companies
- Help people before they start a business – A mentor to guide them
- Don't just pour in money – entrepreneurs must have a viable plan + realise this aid is not meant to go to large established firms
- Promoting change of ownership in family-owned businesses
- Help entrepreneurs expand by easing their managerial capabilities – lower workloads means they can do more
- Each ministry of government support its own colleges – develop its own college courses [why ? because they have more relevant know how] eg. ministry of agriculture supporting colleges of agriculture
- Have entrepreneurship skills included in all college courses
- Colleges setting up their own businesses
- An entrepreneurship college course – if you complete it you will receive a grant towards setting up your planned business / receive tools if your business is a trade. The course should last for two and half years. You might have to get technical assistance from people in other countries to set up these courses. Concentrate on industries where there is most growth potential. Get students to group together to set up a business.

- If a company is getting parts / raw materials cheaply to manufacture a product – import those same parts / raw materials yourself and set up your own business to produce the same competing products within the country.

- Cloning products produced in other countries / by other companies such as in the chemical/pharmaceutical industry // food sector // electronics [computers etc.]

- Tariffs need to be looked at if they are adding costs to other industries in the country that could create more employment

- If there are tariffs – products produced indigenously will be higher than abroad and so will restrict exports & production in this area will be limited to domestic demand

- "Offshoring" – Have companies set up to manufacture [cheaply] ideas of entrepreneurs / companies form other companies

- If you are a processing industry you can import raw materials without taxes of any kind

- The higher the product value change [from raw materials to product] the more profits you can keep

- Advertise your industry policies abroad – contact companies – hold investment/trade fairs in other countries – say what skills/incentives you have

- Different companies marketing their products together under a single brand name : It will be easier for such an association to get credit as a group + After a while individual companies in the association may grow bigger and be able to market themselves individually + Bigger companies are more likely to be able to export

- If a company is producing a product at a cheaper price than abroad – invest more in it/develop it more

- Small companies joining together to form a larger company. They would have more market access and more profits and could grow more and employ more. can compete on the international market more effectively

- Talk to businesses – "What are your plans – how can we help you?" don't wait for them to come to you – government employment agency can do this

- Sister cities – trade delegations from both sides – import from export to

- Feedback from companies if they don't invest in your country / location – why they did not choose you

- A university run by businesses – training students [big companies] – teaching students to run businesses in college
- Incubate companies in college – support them here – develop companies in college
- Training students in vocational secondary schools in skill areas – more than one – student's earn a small wage while in school on the courses
- "Job fairs" – for SME's – to hire students outside of college – grouped by sector
- Training for unemployed where people are placed in jobs for a fixed period to gain work experience / just like students in college
- A support system to set up new business
- Universities develop an idea and get business to take it up in return for employing people from the college / business sponsor more R&D in universities
- College businesses with college financing
- Special financing for new types [sector] industries in a country
- Lower taxes for hiring young people [youth unemployment is particularly high in MENA countries]
- Higher wages for higher skills - encourage people to go for training [in public sector at least] their wages increase if they improve their skills / training relevant to the company - state pays whatever your wag is while you are on training
- Pay a supplement to families for children [per child] to attend secondary school [it doesn't have to be big] - target poor areas for this [improve educational standards of nation]
- Where you already have access to foreign markets - develop related industries to export more there
- **Education :**
- A training association for maths and science teachers A centre for talented student
- Social participation of students in the community
- Make education relevant to employment need
- Education in agricultural studies - agriculture is an asset and must be developed
- **Business**
- Joint action between businesses and education in secondary school
- New business ventures - talk to school pupils / college students help forming curricula for pupils
- Devaluation of currency Get rid of patronage
- State subsidies need to be examined

- Government is taking the best skilled people - freeze the growth in employment here - perhaps then these skilled people will turn to the private sector
- Reward people who create jobs – employers themselves can earn an income personally without having to pay taxes up to a certain level themselves
- Freeze on new employment in government - Increase wages though of those who are employed
- Make it easy to set up a business - One single form to fill out to set up a business - One tax form for yourself and for each employees
- State grants – If a business commits to creating 50 jobs and it does they will receive the grant to boost their business even further
- Employment for students in college while they are in college for a year - experience - at a reduced wage - relevant to their course

Set up new state companies and then sell them off

- What you are strong at reform to make even stronger
- Get them to reinvest in their business [profits] [for businesses under 200 employees] - match their investments dollar for dollar
- A state bank for small businesses - no interest loans + long term payback - [if they fold and start again they must still pay back the original loan]
- Allow private sector to hire and fire people more easily - if they are unviable they will close and will not grow

Re-invest in industries you were strong in in the past - redevelop them - the skills may still be there for them - states can work here

- Partners - Government / business ventures - hand over control of business after a certain number of years. Joint ventures with both foreign companies and indigenous companies – they keep most of the profits – you absorb any losses – a Win – Win situation for them;
- Fiscal rectitude - allow for budget tracking by NGO's / CSO's - This is important there is considerable room for improvement in government spending

Keep your social welfare payments when go to college if over a certain age

- Develop industries add on value - agriculture / oil / tourism

A training agency for skills - can receive social welfare while on courses

- Increase indirect taxes – VAT, DIRT [tax on interest earned on bank accounts], SALES TAX; to replace all other forms of employer taxes
- Minimum wage levels in return for no strikes – people will choose jobs outside the public sector if you do
- No taxes based on number of those you employ base it on profits 10% – 40%
- Informal sector :

- A simple contract for those in informal work :
- agreed work time
- minimum wage for sector [agricultural; labourer; manufacturer etc.];
- get given priority in hiring the next time;

- take a job make a business out of it;
- provide technical colleges with training that address the needs of the informal sector in creating more employment
- "where the jobs are train them"
- Reduce tax rates for those who employ more - proportionately
- You have to realise you cannot continue to rely on the public sector to the absorb the workforce in the future anymore
- One agency for SME's for dealing with all aspects of exporting – deal with company within two months

ON ISLAM

Purpose : To improve peoples understanding of Muslims and how good they actually are.

Strategy : Suggest a "Hearts and Minds" programme of investment by the west in certain Muslim countries to counteract the development of extremism. To provide general information on Muslims and correct misperceptions. To provide advice on how to relate to Muslims. Encourage people to relate to Muslims in a good way. Encourage western leaders to reach out to Muslims in Muslim countries by acknowledging the suffering they have endured.

KEYWORDS

"Good Qualities About Muslims" "Islam Correcting Misperceptions" "Relating To Islam Advice" "Info On Islam" "Hearts And Minds Programmes" "The Hijab"

PAUL ARMSTRONG - MUSLIM GIRLS - THE HIJAB

29/05/2015

Dear Ambassador Thebault,

Please pass the following on to your government.

Dear Sirs / Madams,

I know in the last few years your government left the decision as to whether young muslim girls could wear the hijab in school up to the individual schools principals. In general no one forced these girls to wear the Hijab - they chose to do so out of their own free will.. Wearing the hijab does not offend other girls or their teachers. However if a school has decided to ban the hijab it is a suppression of their religion. France is supposed to be an open and tolerant society. No religious expression is claimed to be egalitarian IT IS NOT; it is discrimination. Leave the decision as to whether to wear the Hijab up to the individual girls and not principals. This would require a very small change in France's laws.

HEARTS AND MINDS PROGRAMMES

This is really important. I want to save the world - now I am concerned about the levels of poverty in some Islamic nations - which needs to be alleviated. I want a peaceful Islam - I want to bring out the best in Islam and I want it to be friends with west. You really need to empower people there and the best way to do it is with "Hearts and Minds programmes" - this is where you provide the financing and local communities decide how it is spent - whether it be health centres, credit unions, facilities for helping the elderly etc. I cannot stress enough how important hearts and minds programmes are in turning a people towards peace and moderatism. I don't want a rise in extremism which is what might fill the vacuum of poverty and unemployment in some Islamic nations - this needs to be avoided. We are talking serious finances here - a major operation. I would replace investments in military aid and training with hearts and minds programmes that would be more likely to engender a happy peaceful stable society. Start with Iran, Egypt and Yemen and Algeria. We are talking in the billions here at least. Far cheaper than the cost of military expenditure in the region!

INFO ON ISLAM

- Muslims are ordinary people – if you ask them what they want – they say the same things as everyone else does – a house, a job a wife
- You should meet with Muslims and talk to them and only then make up your mind and decide how you see Islam
- Outside homes Muslim women may have their rights controlled but in the home their are no restrictions on them not even in the clothes they wear
- Just like the west there are some really good people in Islam
- Surprise, surprise – The family of Osama Bin Laden wanted nothing to do with him – They do not support violence at all. Basically they saw him as a jerk
- If you want to get in a Muslims good books reach out to them in charity
- Muslims have families!
- Muslims have endured a lot of suffering at hands of others | Muslims have encountered persecution in the west – graffiti on Mosque walls / prejudice in the media / stereotyping / hostility from individuals including negative statements from those who claim to be "True Christians"
- Hezbollah / Hamas they want to be talked to / They want to be heard and it may help peace to do so
- Many Muslims believe that in the end times all people will become one and pray one prayer
- Muslims like talking about their own religion and other peoples Christian religions with them

- **CORRECTING MISPERCEPTIONS**

- Women are suppressed re: the wearing of clothes – In fact women in Islam freely choose to wear modest clothing including the veil "Hijab" – they say it liberates them from having to compete for appearances
- Women live isolated lives – In fact most women in Islam have many female friends and enjoy a rich family life / extended family life : family life is central to most Muslims. Eating, dancing well into the night is not uncommon in family homes among friends and family.
- Muslim women are usually illiterate – In fact this is a misperception – The media focuses on illiteracy in Muslim women but this is in third world countries where levels of illiteracy in places like Somalia and Pakistan are the same as wherever else in the third world.
- Their is a misperception in the west that Islam is a violent reiigion and does not have examples of peacemakers. This is quite untrue. I will give you some examples
- Bediuzzaman Said Nursi who lived from 1876 - 1960 was a muslim reformer in Turkey he worked with alot of people - he promoted peace, tolerance, social reform. He was very popular. He affected the lives of millions of people. his work continues today under the auspices of Fethullah Gulen
- The Peace Education Program NGO [Program Pendidikan Damai] - which has worked on educating students in Aceh while there was a conflict there and since in peace education
- The Afghan Institute Of Learning NGO - lead by Sakena Yacoobi which works on educating young girls they worked even during the rule of the Taliban at great risk to themselves
- Abdul Ghaffar Khan - who lived from 1890 - 1988 Khan was a non-violent protester against the British colonial rule
- Soraya Jamjuree - She founded the "Frieds Of Victimized Families NGO who work for reconciliation between muslims and Bhuddhists in South Thailand
- Dakena Ibrahim Abdi - She along with others founded the Wajir Peace And Development Committee NGO which has worked for peace between religiona and warring factions in Kenya, Somalia, Ethiopia, Sudan, Uganda and other parts of the world
- Islam is not a monolithic religion - it is as diverse as Christianity : there are ethnic, national, tribal, linguistic and sectarian differences. Our perceptions of them are shaped by a small minority of highly visible Muslims in the media.
- The majority of Muslims are not arabs - over 80% of them are not arabs. The top four nations with Muslim populations :- India, Indonesia, Pakistan and Bangladesh are not arabs.
- Christian missionaries in Islam do not need to be secretive about their work. Muslims respect courage and honesty even if they disagree and argue against them. Secretive missionaries get followed by the secret police.

ADVICE

- Visit a mosque – Muslims appreciate this
- Give a gift to your host – gift giving is very appreciated in Islam
- Do charitable works for Muslims – make donations to local Muslim charities
- Offer to pray for Muslims you meet
- Apologise for western flaws – promiscuity / lack of morals / materialism
- Acknowledge to Muslims that their feelings of hurt are real and that you want to be friends
- Apologise for Iraq / Palestine / Syria : and say that you want to help – ask for forgiveness
- Never assume you know what a Muslim believes
- Don't talk politics with a Muslim
- Talk about your family and theirs
- Ask them about Islam
- Assume that they are more religious than you

AFFIRM GOOD QUALITIES ABOUT MUSLIMS

- Muslims are good people
- Muslims are more tolerant of Christianity than you realise.
- That Muslims are very generous people
- Muslims truly respect Christians who practice their faith – They have a perception that people in the west have no faith

[SAMPLE LETTER]

Dear Sir / Madam, write a letter and get it published in the national media of Muslim countries apologising for the Wests treatment of Islam – apologising for Iraq; for not doing more to bring peace to the Palestinians. Ask them for forgiveness say you want to help and become friends with Islam. That their hurts are real and justified. That the media in the west should show more respect for Islam. [These are not just meant to be just words – They are to be real!!]

POVERTY IDEAS

27/07/2015

Dear Trocaire,

I hope you find the ideas here helpful. They are to do with social justice and improving the lot of poor people. I will be sending the emails to the UK embassy in Haiti to pass on to prime minister Evans Paul. It will take 1.5 years to work through all the ideas with him. While I am using this for Haiti – you could use for other countries such as in the Caribbean.

EDUCATION

- School feeding programs for children - parents will be more willing to send their children to school.
- Give young children school uniforms [ask another government such as France to sponsor this – ASK FOR THE HELP] - A study in South Africa found that giving uniforms [especially to young girls] increased the likelihood of children staying in school. So they marry at a later age and there are reduced pregnancies
- Exemptions from all school fees for children in poorer municipalities.
- International schools funded by the UN for poor people – at least some will benefit from this
- College students must spend a term working for an NGO - compulsory as part of their degree course
- Politicians attending graduation day for schools from poor student backgrounds
- Free children's books for rural areas - to help children to learn

POLITICS

- Bonus seats for large parties [there are too many small parties in Haiti]
- A congress of Caribbean / Central American nations – on peace, development and social justice
- Double voting for minorities
- Wives of husbands who are elected can be included in parliament - without themselves having to be elected
- Lower the voting age for people - young people are more idealistic
- A passport / visa free area for all Caribbean Central American countries
- Civil Society / NGO's can run for election as parties/individuals - Stay independent of other parties
- Mandatory involvement of NGO's in municipal and local planning and budgeting oversight

- Have to retire from politics when over a certain age - get rid of the old block
- A fast-track court for political crimes [killing of politicians / civil society members]
- After an agreement on reforms – both sides [NGO group / Government] in negotiations visit European other developed nations governments explaining the reforms to get aid to finance the deal
- Develop meeting places – where Haitians can regularly discuss politics, voice complaints – Your government should choose politicians to attend these meetings
- Children write letters to President Michel - there hopes and criticisms. Winning essays from each school are passed on to the president.
- The president cannot be a leader of a political party [can be a member of it though]
- "Mandate parties" campaigning around an issue – religion / political reform / employment / corruption etc
- Set up a democracy institute for Haiti and the rest of the world
- Embassy officials of different governments can question government ministers
- Set trade unionists to join politics

GOVERNMENT

- Recruitment by merit - An employment agency to ensure this rather than quotas. Encourage minorities to apply for jobs through advertising [compulsory]. Agency publishes ethnic quality levels annually

D'Hondt Method

In this example, 230,000 voters decide the disposition of 8 seats among 4 parties. Since 8 seats are to be allocated, divide each party's total votes by 1, then by 2, 3, 4, 5, 6, 7, and 8. The 8 highest entries, marked with asterisks, range from 100,000 down to 25,000. For each, the corresponding party gets a seat. For comparison, the "True proportion" column shows the fractional numbers of seats due, calculated in proportion to the number of votes received. (For example, 100,000/230,000 × 8 = 3.48) The slight favouring of the largest party over the smallest is apparent.

denominator	/1	/2	/3	/4	/5	/6	/7	/8	Seats won (*)	True proportion
Party A	100,000*	50,000*	33,333*	25,000*	20,000	16,666	14,286	12,500	4	3.48
Party B	80,000*	40,000*	26,666*	20,000	16,000	13,333	11,428	10,000	3	2.78
Party C	30,000*	15,000	10,000	7,500	6,000	5,000	4,286	3,750	1	1.04
Party D	20,000	10,000	6,666	5,000	4,000	3,333	2,857	2,500	0	0.70

Table and text under the creative commons license http://creativecommons.org/licenses/by-sa/3.0/

D'Hondt Method : https://en.wikipedia.org/wiki/D%27Hondt-method

COMMUNITY

- Each community appointing leaders to engage with the other communities - hold conferences together - form a commitment to action
- Haitian emigrants returning home to visit old friends
- Feast day meals 3-4 times a year - free food and drink for all provided by landlords
- Relatives of a person can gain ownership of property - A simple form - no bills - while the person is still alive – so old people can move into "granny flats" and families into the houses
- A "LARGE" government NGO fund to finance NGO projects.
- Someone in the village such as a teacher - reads the news in the newspapers to those who are illiterate
- Giving young children a shelter they can use as an address with their own individual postal box
- Reward those involved in social justice
- Indigenous NGO's going abroad to tell the stories of peasants and poor children to international media
- Philanthropy Unions - of rich people and rich companies

YOUTH

- Encourage poor children to aspire to a better life - bring people of different professions to talk to gatherings of poor children in schools
- Organize sports competitions for poor children - give them something of a childhood
- Collective protests where children have been taken into bonded labour to pay bills - supported by politicians

MEDIA

- People who emigrated due to need for income write back to newspapers in Haiti - what they would like to see happen there
- Publicise threats to people in the national media and profile them
- Media can criticise the president / government
- Must be respect for religion in media - A right of response for religious in media
- Right of response for government to media articles
- Allow in foreign media outlets such as the BBC Worldservice
- Haitian media can have branches in other countries
- Journalists may have access to detailed accounts of government spending

Laws And Libel Laws

- A centre of journalists, religious, business, university professors to draw up media laws
- Incitement to hatred between different ethnic groups must be against the law
- Respect for religion provided it is not extreme
- Journalists must not be censored for expressing an opinion
- Parliamentary cross-party committees on investigations into journalists being persecuted / killed
- In libel laws burden of proof must lie with the complainant rather than the journalist
- One third of broadcasting licenses must go to community media
- Cannot refer to ethnic identities within the media
- A human rights commission to regulate journalism
- No businesses can control more than 10% of the media

Purpose of Media

- To hold officials to account by acting as a "watchdog" that brings misuses of power or policy failures to the knowledge of the public
- To provide citizens with the information they need to participate in society
- To serve as a forum for different views both official and alternative - to mobilise support for a cause
- The media must be a moral agency
- The role of the media is to expand knowledge and overcome biases

Media Diversity

- Newspapers can publish contradictory articles journalists on each side taking a side on an issue
- In elections newspapers television must publish the goals of all political parties as they are written
- Political party assemblies to ensure that party political policies are more than just a rubberstamp for leaders

- A "nationwide" programme to highlight good works being done all around the country
- A Reuters style news agency for Haiti - government financed - run by national journalists union - insist on factual / accurate news reporting from the agency
- Allow public relations companies

Corruption

- There must be a separation between media ownership and editorial decision-making
- To deal with bribes in journalism - journalists can look for support from editors
- Media assistance body to deal with corruption in journalism

POVERTY

- Talk about poverty in all classrooms - what is/has been done about it in Haiti
- Haitian expatriates in USA and other major countries send "remittances" to Haitian municpality offices. The money is used for development projects. Civil society are involved in these projects. Haitian government matches money on a three to one basis. Look at the example of Mexico. The municipality inform migrants of projects developed.
- Government provides a "LARGER" grant in place of regular social assistance payments to poor people five to six times a year. – Since government cannot afford regular social welfare
- Cancel all debts owed by peasants to the government "an amnesty"
- Husbands / wives of prime ministers taking up social causes
- A peasants institute – for policy development / research / empowering peasants

BUSINESS

- A law against monopolization in financial / agricultural / commercial and mining sectors :- break up industries if necessary

LAND

- Government leasing land from landlords to give to peasants :- long-term leases : eventually they own the land
- Allow groups of small farmers to take out a loan together – and if they pay back the loan in full – they can then apply for a bigger loan
- Designating agricultural land use in certain areas – prevent landholders from appropriating land and using it for cattle ranching [which requires very few workers]
- Add women's names to land titles alongside their husbands names
- Digital registry of all lands owned by peasants
- If as a peasant you have been on the land for a number of years the land becomes yours
- Agricultural colleges / local courses in the villages [a few weeks]

- Middlemen agree to pay a certain wage to peasants at start of planting season - the payment is guaranteed
- Auctioning of produce to middlemen by peasants to get the best prices
- Unused land must be sold to peasants
- Landlords can pay their tenants in land rather than money
- A lead farm - introducing new techniques [trained by government - they then pass this knowledge onto other farmers
- The eldest son / daughter inherits the land - cannot keep breaking up the land into smaller proportions
- Landlords must give one months salary to landless labourers when they are no longer needed
- Zoning agricultural land - more food for people less cash crops
- Very long term low interest loans [30 - 40 years] from the government to peasants to buy their land
- Landlords incomes will be tax free if they sell their land [incentive for them to sell to peasants]
- If landlords do not live on land they must sell it to the government
- Maybe government cannot provide lands but houses for landless can be built on landlords land where they work.- co-funding between landlords and government

JUSTICE
- Broadcast criminal trials of corrupt politicians / military abuses on television
- Get mayors in each city to publish crime statistics. This will prevent hard-line city councillors from rejecting further police reforms and from abandoning current reforms. Publicise data at press conferences / community briefings / newsletters
- Community meetings which are attended by police officials where citizens discuss how the police could be more accountable to city residents. This forces the police to engage in dialogue with varied social sectors that it has long lacked accountability to + forcing hard-line politicians in city councils to accept further reforms
- Local communities involved in recruiting members to the police force
- If politicians made trafficking and bonded labour a national issue the police would be forced to act
- Arrest the customers who use brothels not the girls / women
- Investigate armed groups maintained by Landlords after an amnesty on the issue - charge those who still maintain them
- A day of mourning for people who have suffered from violence due to their social justice efforts - Politicians attending these meetings and pledging to make reforms

URBAN
- Rank cities / towns for their level of adherence to poverty indicators

- Access points in cities for people to get clean water

THE CHURCH
- A Catholic radio station
- Roman Catholic Church intervening at crucial stages where there is disagreement and they make the decision
- Catholic church attend meetings between government and NGO's as an observer

WOMEN
- A woman's night out on the town : only women allowed on the city centre streets [no men] – Colombia has done this
- In seeking justice for women abused / raped - they should ask a local politician to go with them to the police
- A university for women
- Training midwifes for each village at least two of them in each village

POLITICAL CORRUPTION LETTER
Dear Mr President,

I'll be honest - my personal opinion is that you have been involved in corruption to one degree or another. You have a decent standard of living compared to the rest of your people. I also suspect that you are providing money to your party politicians to keep them loyal. This is heavy criticism I know but what if it is true. I would put an amnesty [confidential] for past corruption - provided politicians end corrupt activities. It is a sin to be involved in corruption. Can you accept that it is a sin. I am sorry for saying these things and I don't want to threaten your position as president. Corrupt regimes keep people in poverty with just an elite class being wealthy. There will be change - I believe you if you say you will tackle corruption. The west is going to have to help countries like you improve the living standards of everyone. You have sinned - maybe you don't like hearing this but I think it is true. There has to be change - eliminate corruption in politics and businesses please. This was a difficult letter to write but I had to do it.

STUDENT'S SPEAKING OUT
Dear Mr President

Allow NGO's to speak at third level colleges. Allow debates in universities on anything from democracy to education. Commemorating people who have died and worked for social justice - Speeches given in universities / school halls. Your party politicians attending these meetings and assuring people they can speak out and that they are safe to do so. Politics does involve pressure on those elected; without it you would be a dictatorship. Students are the future of your country and independent thinking should be encouraged. Do you get the feeling that people are not being genuine to you - if no one can criticise you, your are a dictatorship. Is there a sharp divide between the people and politicians - their right to choose who represents them if this is so you could be described as a dictatorship. You should compare yourself to those around you other countries - how do they treat their people. How do you stand in relation to them. Do others describe you as a dictatorship - if they do then there must be substantial and committed hanges. A new era for Haiti - you might not always be president indeed no politician should ever be president for life. The typical standard abroad is two terms of seven years and then no more - if this is not so you are raising concerns about being a dictatorship.

MILITARY LETTER

To The Chief Of Staff Of The Defence Forces - Reducing Military Budget - Keeping Military Busy

Dear Sir, I think your president is moving towards a democracy - Now in other countries particularly in Africa when the power of the military is reduced in many cases a coup d'etat erupts. This should not be so for Haiti - A responsible military must recognise that it cannot be involved in politics. You have important responsibility in ensuring peace is maintained - no matter who is president [elections]. Soldiers are brave people. They would follow your orders [keep the peace]. In some cases the military is a business such as in the USA that is not good. Asking you to accept cuts in your budget is necessary as you make peace with the countries around you. More resources can be spent on your people as a result. Generally where the military does not exercise too much power - you have stable governments and like my own country more can be spent on looking after the people. One area of suggestion is that Haiti contribute peacekeeping forces to the UN. Keeping the peace [again] only this time in another country. Generally other countries in the wealthier west contribute to the costs of such operations so there is no danger of the government reducing aid assistance to your people to support the military. You could also become involved in joint military training with a country in the west

CORRUPTION

- Invite bureaucrats to people's kitchens - less likely to be involved in corruption if they get to know the locals
- A branch within the police specifically to investigate corruption
- Get individual politicians across the political divide [different parties] to join together on combating corruption
- Business surveys to highlight levels of corruption
- Business can fill out government forms over the internet to avoid levels of corruption
- Politicians have to declare all their income sources [including you Mr. President]
- Media publicising corruption
- Rewards for reporting corruption if it shows to be true

- Judges are in charge of appointing senior civil service members
- A business integrity forum - to ensure businesses do not have to give bribes to people.
- Limit the amount of money businesses can give to political parties - all business may only donate to parties and not to individuals
- Politicians can register to have their finances investigated by the judiciary - Establish their credentials as "clean" politicians
- Politicians including the president cannot have shares or ownership over state assets<
- Establish a citizen report card - to survey citizens opinions / experiences of various state companies / state ministries. The results would be publicised in the media
- A UN workshop on corruption for politicians in a country
- A minister for corruption - drawn from civil society
- An international court in the country appointed by the AU to deal with corruption; validating elections - Reasons for this local judiciary is not skilled enough - concerns that local judiciary may not be as efficient due to lack of funding
- International police training for investigations / audits of people's finances
- Community groups - individuals joining together when seeking financing / applications for services - may reduce corruption
- NGO's can talk direct to the president about corruption
- Appointing judiciary with approval of parliament
- The public service proposes expenditure for government and then the government decides on it
- A tracking survey - how much of government funding budgeted for schools, health clinics etc. actually reaches them - citizens monitoring the budget
- Party financing must be made public - who supported them
- Political parties must have a party support base of people | must garner at least 1,000 signatures to form a party
- Political leaders must have their finances investigated
- Party base nominates those who can become politicians after any elections
- Protect those in the civil service who expose corruption
- Media presence at court cases | especially corruption cases
- Media can have access to public service to audit where money is being "lost" along the chain of bureaucracy
- Must vote for a party rather than individual politicians - reduces corruption such as buying votes / politicians doing favours for people
- Reform within the police by the police
- Making people aware of the consequences of corruption. They will be less likely to give in to corruption or accept it
- Force new legislation on corruption by gathering votes from across the political divide in parliament

POLICE CORRUPTION

- Rotating police officers between districts to reduce corruption
- Vary police officers roles
- Full screening of backgrounds of recruits to the police force
- Candidates with higher levels of education should be sought and those who continue their education should be rewarded
- A use of a polygraph testing in initial screenings of candidates
- Police commanders are held personally responsible for their subordinates actions with regard to corruption
- Community policing begins after extensive training where police officers spend several days conducting surveys at each residence and business in their assigned neighborhood. There are two purposes for this 1. To introduce police officers to community residences and generate public interest 2. They provide officers with a preliminary assessment of the principal concerns specific to the community - providing info not just on citizen security but other social problems as well.
- An external commission to monitor police - independent of governance; must publicize findings
- Start from the top down. Police commanders must be seen visibly and persistently to lead reform
- Reinforce the message by personal visits to the rank and file police stations
- Reformers must think of ways to remind officers about what is expected in particular situations
- Signs can be placed at receiving counters at police stations that complaints must be registered without monetary charge
- Police should develop programs informing the public about anti-corruption initiatives and publicize procedures for complaining - This may raise anxiety among police officers that people will complain
- Police showing sincere efforts at reform will gain more respect from the public - giving them a sense of pride. Policing then becomes a vocation rather than a job
- Bring together police officer and civil society representatives to overcome a legacy of suspicion and fear. Participants in these dialogues exchange information about the sources of crime and violence and discussed ways that the police best re-establish control in the community. These dialogues should be renewed and continue

FINANCES

- A 5% tax for the poor on the middle and upper classes similar to the Muslim system of Zakat[5% also]
- A one-time wealth tax – for construction purposes
- Indigenous NGO's establishing offices in western countries for fundraising
- Get the president of Haiti involved - he should have a presidential fund which he can use to help others such as women and children

- Village leaders with more powers can raise a very small tax on local landlords

POVERTY LETTERS

<u>KEYWORDS</u>

"Education" "Politics" "Government" "Community" "Youth" "Media" "Poverty" "Business" "Land" "Justice" "Urban" "The Church" "Women" "Political Corruption" "Military" "Corruption" "Police Corruption" "Finances"

#1 EDUCATION - HAITI - FOR PRIME MINISTER EVANS PAUL - PAUL ARMSTRONG

25/06/2015

Dear Deputy Head Of Mission - Mr. Rick Shearn,

I want to work with you on bringing social justice to Haiti – especially I am concerned with the poor of Haiti. Please can you pass the following email onto Mr Evans Paul – Prime Minister of Haiti. It concerns education in Haiti. I will be sending several more over the course of the next 1.5 years. If you have any ideas yourself [under the topic of the particular email] you can include them too.

Thank You

Dear Prime Minister - Mr Evans Paul

I want to deal with poverty and inequality in your country – I am sure you are just as concerned about it as I am – You just need the right ideas. Over the next 1.5 years I will be sending you emails with ideas for dealing with poverty and inequality. I hope you accept my ideas and implement them. There is a lot of work to be done. I want to empower people and that is the best way to end poverty. The government of your country is going to have to implement these ideas and enforce them – it will not be free of cost but I believe it is possible. My first email is on education. Thank you for taking the time to read this email

<u>EDUCATION</u>

- School feeding programs for children - parents will be more willing to send their children to school.
- Give young children school uniforms [ask another government such as France to sponsor this – ASK FOR THE HELP] - A study in South Africa found that giving uniforms [especially to young

girls] increased the likelihood of children staying in school. So they marry at a later age and there are reduced pregnancies

- Exemptions from all school fees for children in poorer municipalities
- International schools funded by the UN for poor people – at least some will benefit from this
- College students must spend a term working for an NGO - compulsory as part of their degree course
- Politicians attending graduation day for schools from poor student backgrounds
- Free children's books for rural areas - to help children to learn

#2 POLITICS - HAITI - FOR PRIME MINISTER EVANS PAUL - PAUL ARMSTRONG

25/07/2015

Dear Deputy Head Of Mission - Mr. Rick Shearn,

This is my second email to you it concerns politics in Haiti and the reforms I would like to see happen there. I want to work with you on bringing social justice to Haiti – especially I am concerned with the poor of Haiti. Please can you pass the following email onto Mr Evans Paul – Prime Minister of Haiti. I will be sending several more. If you have any ideas yourself [under the topic of the particular email] you can include them too.

Thank You

Dear Prime Minister - Mr Evans Paul,

There is always room for political reform – make politics work better and be closer to the people. Again social justice is my primary concern here. I hope you accept my ideas. There are a lot of them – I don't think anything here will meet with much opposition. I enclose all my previous emails to you. I will write to you again. Thank You for taking the time to read this email.

POLITICS

- Bonus seats for large parties [there are too many small parties in Haiti]
- A congress of Caribbean / Central American nations – on peace, development and social justice
- Double voting for minorities
- Wives of husbands who are elected can be included in parliament - without themselves having to be elected
- Lower the voting age for people - young people are more idealistic   .
- A passport / visa free area for all Caribbean Central American countries
- Civil Society / NGO's can run for election as parties/individuals - Stay independent of other parties

- Mandatory involvement of NGO's in municipal and local planning and budgeting oversight
- Have to retire from politics when over a certain age - get rid of the old block
- A fast-track court for political crimes [killing of politicians / civil society members]
- After an agreement on reforms – both sides [NGO group / Government] in negotiations visit European other developed nations governments explaining the reforms to get aid to finance the deal
- Develop meeting places – where Haitians can regularly discuss politics, voice complaints – Your government should choose politicians to attend these meetings
- Children write letters to President Michel - there hopes and criticisms. Winning essays from each school are passed on to the president.
- The president cannot be a leader of a political party [can be a member of it though]
- "Mandate parties" campaigning around an issue – religion / political reform / employment / corruption etc
- Set up a democracy institute for Haiti and the rest of the world
- Embassy officials of different governments can question government ministers
- Set trade unionists to join politics

#3 GOVERNMENT - HAITI - FOR PRIME MINISTER EVANS PAUL - PAUL ARMSTRONG

25/08/2015

Dear Deputy Head Of Mission - Mr. Rick Shearn,

This is my third email to you it concerns government in Haiti and the reforms I would like to see happen there. I want to work with you on bringing social justice to Haiti – especially I am concerned with the poor of Haiti. Please can you pass the following email onto Mr Evans Paul – Prime Minister of Haiti. I will be sending several more. If you have any ideas yourself [under the topic of the particular email] you can include them too.

Thank You

Dear Prime Minister - Mr Evans Paul,

I am writing to you now about governance in your country. In particular I am proposing a new way of forming governments – governments of grand coalition with parties nominating their ministers in turn according to the size of their vote. What I am referring to is the D'Hondt method of politics – used by many countries. One country of note where it has been done successfully is Northern Ireland. Here I also enclose all my previous emails to you. I will write to you again

Thank you for taking the time to read this email

GOVERNMENT

Recruitment by merit - An employment agency to ensure this rather than quotas. Encourage minorities to apply for jobs through advertising [compulsory]. Agency publishes ethnic quality levels annually

D'Hondt Method

In this example, 230,000 voters decide the disposition of 8 seats among 4 parties. Since 8 seats are to be allocated, divide each party's total votes by 1, then by 2, 3, 4, 5, 6, 7, and 8. The 8 highest entries, marked with asterisks, range from 100,000 down to 25,000. For each, the corresponding party gets a seat. For comparison, the "True proportion" column shows the fractional numbers of seats due, calculated in proportion to the number of votes received. (For example, 100,000/230,000 × 8 = 3.48) The slight favouring of the largest party over the smallest is apparent

denominator	/1	/2	/3	/4	/5	/6	/7	/8	Seats won (*)	True proportion
Party A	100,000*	50,000*	33,333*	25,000*	20,000	16,666	14,286	12,500	4	3.48
Party B	80,000*	40,000*	26,666*	20,000	16,000	13,333	11,428	10,000	3	2.78
Party C	30,000*	15,000	10,000	7,500	6,000	5,000	4,286	3,750	1	1.04
Party D	20,000	10,000	6,666	5,000	4,000	3,333	2,857	2,500	0	0.70

Table under the creative commons license http://creativecommons.org/licenses/by-sa/3.0/
D'Hondt Method : https://en.wikipedia.org/wiki/D'Hondt_method

#4 COMMUNITY - HAITI - FOR PRIME MINISTER EVANS PAUL - PAUL ARMSTRONG

25/09/2015

Dear Deputy Head Of Mission - Mr. Rick Shearn,

This is my fourth email to you it concerns communities in Haiti and the reforms I would like to see happen there. I want to work with you on bringing social justice to Haiti – especially I am concerned with the poor of Haiti. Please can you pass the following email onto Mr Evans Paul –

Prime Minister of Haiti. I will be sending several more. If you have any ideas yourself [under the topic of the particular email] you can include them too

Thank You

Dear Prime Minister – Mr Evans Paul

I enclose my fourth email to you. It provides a range of ideas on community empowerment. All these ideas are feasible and will not cost a lot. Here I also enclose all my previous emails to you. I will write to you again.

Thank You Mr Prime Minister

COMMUNITY

- Each community appointing leaders to engage with the other communities - hold conferences together - form a commitment to action
- Haitian emigrants returning home to visit old friends
- Feast day meals 3-4 times a year - free food and drink for all provided by landlords
- Relatives of a person can gain ownership of property - A simple form - no bills - while the person is still alive – so old people can move into "granny flats" and families into the houses
- A "LARGE" government NGO fund to finance NGO projects.
- Someone in the village such as a teacher - reads the news in the newspapers to those who are illiterate
- Giving young children a shelter they can use as an address with their own individual postal box
- Reward those involved in social justice
- Indigenous NGO's going abroad to tell the stories of peasants and poor children to international media
- Philanthropy Unions - of rich people and rich companies

#5 YOUTH - HAITI - FOR PRIME MINISTER EVANS PAUL - PAUL ARMSTRONG

25/10/2015

Dear Deputy Head Of Mission - Mr. Rick Shearn,

This is my fifth email to you it concerns the youth of Haiti and the reforms I would like to see happen there. I want to work with you on bringing social justice to Haiti – especially I am concerned with the poor of Haiti. Please can you pass the following email onto Mr Evans Paul – Prime Minister of Haiti. I will be sending several more. If you have any ideas yourself [under the topic of the particular email] you can include them too.

Thank You

Dear Prime Minister – Mr Evans Paul

I enclose my fifth email to you. It concerns the youth of Haiti. The reforms here are mainly concerned with making children from poor families happier and to help those without a family – forced to live in shanty towns. I include all my previous emails to you here – I will write to you again.

Thank You Mr Prime Minister

YOUTH

- Encourage poor children to aspire to a better life - bring people of different professions to talk to gatherings of poor children in schools
- Organize sports competitions for poor children - give them something of a childhood
- Collective protests where children have been taken into bonded labour to pay bills - supported by politicians

#6 MEDIA - HAITI - FOR PRIME MINISTER EVANS PAUL - PAUL ARMSTRONG

25/11/2015

Dear Deputy Head Of Mission - Mr. Rick Shearn,

This is my sixth email to you it concerns the media of Haiti and the reforms I would like to see happen there. I want to work with you on bringing social justice to Haiti – especially I am concerned with the poor of Haiti. Please can you pass the following email onto Mr Evans Paul – Prime Minister of Haiti. I will be sending several more. If you have any ideas yourself [under the topic of the particular email] you can include them too.

Thank You

Dear Prime Minister – Mr Evans Paul

I enclose my sixth email to you. It concerns the media in Haiti. The issues covered include laws and libel laws; the purpose of the media; media diversity and corruption in journalism. Many of these ideas can be included in the constitution of Haiti. Here I also enclose all my previous emails to you. Thank you for taking the time to read this email – I will write to you again.

MEDIA

- People who emigrated due to need for income write back to newspapers in Haiti - what they would like to see happen there
- Publicise threats to people in the national media and profile them
- Media can criticise the president / government
- Must be respect for religion in media - A right of response for religious in media

- Right of response for government to media articles
- Allow in foreign media outlets such as the BBC Worldservice
- Haitian media can have branches in other countries
- Journalists may have access to detailed accounts of government spending

Laws And Libel Laws
- A centre of journalists, religious, business, university professors to draw up media laws
- Incitement to hatred between different ethnic groups must be against the law
- Respect for religion provided it is not extreme
- Journalists must not be censored for expressing an opinion
- Parliamentary cross-party committees on investigations into journalists being persecuted / killed
- In libel laws burden of proof must lie with the complainant rather than the journalist
- One third of broadcasting licenses must go to community media
- Cannot refer to ethnic identities within the media
- A human rights commission to regulate journalism
- No businesses can control more than 10% of the media

Purpose of Media
- To hold officials to account by acting as a "watchdog" that brings misuses of power or policy failures to the knowledge of the public
- To provide citizens with the information they need to participate in society
- To serve as a forum for different views both official and alternative - to mobilise support for a cause
- The media must be a moral agency
- The role of the media is to expand knowledge and overcome biases

Media Diversity
- Newspapers can publish contradictory articles journalists on each side taking a side on an issue
- In elections newspapers television must publish the goals of all political parties as they are written
- Political party assemblies to ensure that party political policies are more than just a rubberstamp for leaders
- A "nationwide" programme to highlight good works being done all around the country
- A Reuters style news agency for Haiti - government financed - run by national journalists union - insist on factual / accurate news reporting from the agency
- Allow public relations companies

Corruption

- There must be a separation between media ownership and editorial decision-making
- To deal with bribes in journalism - journalists can look for support from editors
- Media assistance body to deal with corruption in journalism

#7 POVERTY - HAITI - FOR PRIME MINISTER EVANS PAUL - PAUL ARMSTRONG

25/12/2015
Dear Deputy Head Of Mission - Mr. Rick Shearn,
This is my seventh email to you it concerns the poverty in Haiti and the reforms I would like to see happen there. I want to work with you on bringing social justice to Haiti – especially I am concerned with the poor of Haiti. Please can you pass the following email onto Mr Evans Paul – Prime Minister of Haiti. I will be sending several more. If you have any ideas yourself [under the topic of the particular email] you can include them too.
Thank You

Dear Prime Minister – Mr Evans Paul
I enclose my seventh email to you. It concerns the poverty in Haiti. I would strongly recommend you implement the ideas in this email. Here I also enclose all my previous emails to you. Thank you for taking the time to read this email – I will write to you again.

POVERTY
- Talk about poverty in all classrooms - what is/has been done about it in Haiti
- Haitian expatriates in USA and other major countries send "remittances" to Haitian municpality offices. The money is used for development projects. Civil society are involved in these projects. Haitian government matches money on a three to one basis. Look at the example of Mexico. The municipality inform migrants of projects developed.
- Government provides a "LARGER" grant in place of regular social assistance payments to poor people five to six times a year. – Since government cannot afford regular social welfare
- Cancel all debts owed by peasants to the government "an amnesty"
- Husbands / wives of prime ministers taking up social causes
- A peasants institute – for policy development / research / empowering peasants

#8 BUSINESS - HAITI - FOR PRIME MINISTER EVANS PAUL - PAUL ARMSTRONG

25/01/2016

Dear Deputy Head Of Mission - Mr. Rick Shearn,

This is my eighth email to you it concerns the business reform in Haiti. I want to work with you on bringing social justice to Haiti – especially I am concerned with the poor of Haiti. Please can you pass the following email onto Mr Evans Paul – Prime Minister of Haiti. I will be sending several more. If you have any ideas yourself [under the topic of the particular email] you can include them too.

Thank You

Dear Prime Minister – Mr Evans Paul

I enclose my eight email to you. It concerns the business reform in Haiti. This issue is important because very few people benefit from large conglomerates in agriculture / mining etc. Implementing the following idea would lead to greater competition and more people would be employed – empowering more people and bringing them out of poverty. Here I also enclose all my previous emails to you. Thank you for taking the time to read this email – I will write to you again.

BUSINESS

- A law against monopolization in financial / agricultural / commercial and mining sectors :- break up industries if necessary

#9 LAND REFORM HAITI - HAITI - FOR PRIME MINISTER EVANS PAUL - PAUL ARMSTRONG

25/02/2016

Dear Deputy Head Of Mission - Mr. Rick Shearn,

This is my ninth email to you it concerns the land reform in Haiti. I want to work with you on bringing social justice to Haiti – especially I am concerned with the poor of Haiti. Please can you pass the following email onto Mr Evans Paul – Prime Minister of Haiti. I will be sending several more. If you have any ideas yourself [under the topic of the particular email] you can include them too.

Thank You

Dear Prime Minister – Mr Evans Paul

I enclose my ninth email to you. It concerns land rights and land usage in your country. I hope you implement all these ideas even if you encounter some opposition to them from vested interests. The ideas here are probably going to meet some resistance to pass through government. A lot of people with financial interests may oppose you here. But if we are talking about social justice and if you care enough for all the people suffering right now – you will push through this legislation.

LAND

- Government leasing land from landlords to give to peasants :- long-term leases : eventually they own the land
- Allow groups of small farmers to take out a loan together – and if they pay back the loan in full – they can then apply for a bigger loan
- Designating agricultural land use in certain areas – prevent landholders from appropriating land and using it for cattle ranching [which requires very few workers]
- Add women's names to land titles alongside their husbands names
- Digital registry of all lands owned by peasants
- If as a peasant you have been on the land for a number of years the land becomes yours
- Agricultural colleges / local courses in the villages [a few weeks]
- Middlemen agree to pay a certain wage to peasants at start of planting season - the payment is guaranteed
- Auctioning of produce to middlemen by peasants to get the best prices
- Unused land must be sold to peasants
- Landlords can pay their tenants in land rather than money
- A lead farm - introducing new techniques [trained by government - they then pass this knowledge onto other farmers
- The eldest son / daughter inherits the land - cannot keep breaking up the land into smaller proportions
- Landlords must give one months salary to landless labourers when they are no longer needed
- Zoning agricultural land - more food for people less cash crops
- Very long term low interest loans [30 - 40 years] from the government to peasants to buy their land
- Landlords incomes will be tax free if they sell their land [incentive for them to sell to peasants]
- If landlords do not live on land they must sell it to the government
- Maybe government cannot provide lands but houses for landless can be built on landlords land where they work.- co-funding between landlords and government

#10 JUSTICE - HAITI - FOR PRIME MINISTER EVANS PAUL - PAUL ARMSTRONG

25/03/2016

Dear Deputy Head Of Mission - Mr. Rick Shearn,

This is my tenth email to you it concerns justice issues in Haiti. I want to work with you on bringing social justice to Haiti – especially I am concerned with the poor of Haiti. Please can you pass the following email onto Mr Evans Paul – Prime Minister of Haiti. I will be sending several more. If you have any ideas yourself [under the topic of the particular email] you can include them too.

Thank You

Dear Prime Minister – Mr Evans Paul

I enclose my tenth email to you. It concerns justice issues in your country – dealing with those who abuse their positions. In particular it deals with reasons to improve policing and criminal matters. The ideas below are not going to cost a lot but they are good ideas. I enclose all my previous emails to you. Thank you for taking the time to read this email – I will write to you again.

JUSTICE

- Broadcast criminal trials of corrupt politicians / military abuses on television
- Get mayors in each city to publish crime statistics. This will prevent hard-line city councillors from rejecting further police reforms and from abandoning current reforms. Publicise data at press conferences / community briefings / newsletters
- Community meetings which are attended by police officials where citizens discuss how the police could be more accountable to city residents. This forces the police to engage in dialogue with varied social sectors that it has long lacked accountability to + forcing hard-line politicians in city councils to accept further reforms
- Local communities involved in recruiting members to the police force
- If politicians made trafficking and bonded labour a national issue the police would be forced to act
- Arrest the customers who use brothels not the girls / women
- Investigate armed groups maintained by Landlords after an amnesty on the issue - charge those who still maintain them
- A day of mourning for people who have suffered from violence due to their social justice efforts - Politicians attending these meetings and pledging to make reforms

#11 URBAN - HAITI - FOR PRIME MINISTER EVANS PAUL - PAUL ARMSTRONG

25/04/2016

Dear Deputy Head Of Mission - Mr. Rick Shearn,

This is my eleventh email to you it concerns simple urban issues in Haiti. I want to work with you on bringing social justice to Haiti – especially I am concerned with the poor of Haiti. Please can you pass the following email onto Mr Evans Paul – Prime Minister of Haiti. I will be sending several more. If you have any ideas yourself [under the topic of the particular email] you can include them too.

Thank You

Dear Prime Minister – Mr Evans Paul

I enclose my eleventh email to you. I am writing here to you concerning simple to implement urban issues. Firstly people need clean water – something which many in shanty towns do not get and secondly it concerns rating cities according to how much they invest in dealing with poverty issues. I enclose all my previous emails to you. I will write to you again.

<u>URBAN</u>
- Rank cities / towns for their level of adherence to poverty indicators
- Access points in cities for people to get clean water

#12 THE CATHOLIC CHURCH - HAITI - FOR PRIME MINISTER EVANS PAUL - PAUL ARMSTRONG

25/05/2016

Dear Deputy Head Of Mission - Mr. Rick Shearn,

This is my twelfth email to you it concerns the Catholic church and how they can help Haiti. I want to work with you on bringing social justice to Haiti – especially I am concerned with the poor of Haiti. Please can you pass the following email onto Mr Evans Paul – Prime Minister of Haiti. I will be sending several more. If you have any ideas yourself [under the topic of the particular email] you can include them too.

Thank You

Dear Prime Minister – Mr Evans Paul

I enclose my twelfth email to you. It concerns the Catholic church in Haiti and what it can do to help in negotiations between NGO's and government on social reforms. The Catholic church is a force for good in the world AND if you are a religious man which I hope you are then you would approve of these few ideas. There are going to have to be negotiations with NGO's – on a program of reforms. I also enclose all my previous emails to you. I will write to you again.

THE CHURCH

- A Catholic radio station
- Roman Catholic Church intervening at crucial stages where there is disagreement and they make the decision
- Catholic church attend meetings between government and NGO's as an observer

#13 WOMEN - HAITI - FOR PRIME MINISTER EVANS PAUL - PAUL ARMSTRONG

25/06/2016

Dear Deputy Head Of Mission - Mr. Rick Shearn,

This is my thirteenth email to you it concerns improving the quality of women's lives. I want to work with you on bringing social justice to Haiti – especially I am concerned with the poor of Haiti. Please can you pass the following email onto Mr Evans Paul – Prime Minister of Haiti. I will be sending several more. If you have any ideas yourself [under the topic of the particular email] you can include them too. I enclose all my previous correspondence to you.

Thank You

Dear Prime Minister – Mr Evans Paul

I enclose my thirteenth email to you. It predominantly concerns quality of life for women. The ideas are simple and some quite novel such as a university for women only. Thank you for taking the time to read this email – I enclose all my previous correspondence to you. I will write to you again.

WOMEN

- A woman's night out on the town : only women allowed on the city centre streets [no men] – Colombia has done this
- In seeking justice for women abused / raped - they should ask a local politician to go with them to the police
- A university for women
- Training midwifes for each village at least two of them in each village

#14 POLITICAL CORRUPTION - HAITI - FOR PRIME MINISTER EVANS PAUL - PAUL ARMSTRONG

25/07/2016

Dear Deputy Head Of Mission - Mr. Rick Shearn,

This is my fourteenth email to you it concerns corruption in politics. I want to work with you on bringing social justice to Haiti – especially I am concerned with the poor of Haiti. Please can you pass the following email onto Mr Evans Paul – Prime Minister of Haiti. I will be sending several more. If you have any ideas yourself [under the topic of the particular email] you can include them too. I enclose all my previous correspondence to you.

Thank You

Dear Prime Minister – Mr Evans Paul

I enclose my fourteenth email to you. I'll be honest - my personal opinion is that you have been involved in corruption to one degree or another. You have a decent standard of living compared to the rest of your people. I also suspect that you are providing money to your party politicians to keep them loyal. This is heavy criticism I know but what if it is true. I would put an amnesty [confidential] for past corruption - provided politicians end corrupt activities. It is a sin to be involved in corruption.. I am sorry for saying these things and I don't want to threaten your position as prime minister. Corrupt regimes keep people in poverty with just an elite class being wealthy. There will be change - I believe you if you say you will tackle corruption. The west is going to have to help countries like you improve the living standards of everyone. There has to be change - eliminate corruption in politics and businesses please. This was a difficult letter to write but I had to do it. I enclose all my previous correspondence to you – I will write to you again.

#15 STUDENT'S SPEAKING OUT / CONTROLLED GOVERNMENT - HAITI - FOR PRIME MINISTER EVANS PAUL - PAUL ARMSTRONG

25/08/2016

Dear Deputy Head Of Mission - Mr. Rick Shearn,

This is my fifteenth email to you it concerns freedom of expression and debating in particular for students and whether the term dictatorship applies to the Haiti government. I want to work with you on bringing social justice to Haiti – especially I am concerned with the poor of Haiti. Please can you pass the following email onto Mr Evans Paul – Prime Minister of Haiti. I will be sending several more. If you have any ideas yourself [under the topic of the particular email] you can include them too. I enclose all my previous correspondence to you.

Thank You

Dear Prime Minister – Mr Evans Paul

I enclose my fifteenth email to you. Allow NGO's to speak at third level colleges. Allow debates in universities on anything from democracy to education. Commemorating people who have died and worked for social justice - Speeches given in universities / school halls. Your party politicians attending these meetings and assuring people they can speak out and that they are safe to do so. Politics does involve pressure on those elected; without it you would be a dictatorship. Students are the future of your country and independent thinking should be encouraged. Do you get the feeling that people are not being genuine to you - if no one can criticise you, your are a dictatorship. Is there a sharp divide between the people and politicians - their right to choose who represents them if this is so you could be described as a dictatorship. You should compare yourself to those around you other countries - how do they treat their people. How do you stand in relation to them. Do others describe you as a dictatorship - if they do then there must be substantial and committed changes. A new era for Haiti - you might not always be president indeed no politician should ever be president for life. The typical standard abroad is two terms of seven years and then no more - if this is not so you are raising concerns about being a dictatorship.

#16 MILITARY - HAITI - FOR PRIME MINISTER EVANS PAUL - PAUL ARMSTRONG

25/09/2016

Dear Deputy Head Of Mission - Mr. Rick Shearn,

This is my sixteenth email to you it concerns the military in Haiti and how it should act in a democracy. I want to work with you on bringing social justice to Haiti – especially I am concerned with the poor of Haiti. Please can you pass the following email onto Mr Evans Paul – Prime Minister of Haiti. I will be sending several more. If you have any ideas yourself [under the topic of the particular email] you can include them too. I enclose all my previous correspondence to you.

Thank You

Dear Prime Minister – Mr Evans Paul

I enclose my sixteenth email to you. Can you pass this email on to the Chief Of Staff of the defence forces. Don't be afraid of what is written below – I am confident your position and your government are safe but this email is just to keep the military on course – They should not be involved in politics. I will write to you again – I also enclose all my previous correspondence to you.

Dear Sir, I think your president is moving towards a democracy - Now in other countries particularly in Africa when the power of the military is reduced in many cases a coup d'etat erupts. This should not be so for Haiti - A responsible military must recognise that it cannot be involved in politics. You have important responsibility in ensuring peace is maintained - no matter who is president [elections]. Soldiers are brave people. They would follow your orders [keep the peace]. In some cases the military is a business such as in the USA that is not good. Asking you to accept cuts in your budget is necessary as you make peace with the countries around you. More resources can be spent on your people as a result. Generally where the military does not exercise too much power - you have stable governments and like my own country more can be spent on looking after the people. One area of suggestion is that Haiti contribute peacekeeping forces to the UN. Keeping the peace [again] only this time in another country. Generally other countries in the wealthier west contribute to the costs of such operations so there is no danger of the government reducing aid assistance to your people to support the military. You could also become involved in joint military training with a country in the west.

#17 CORRUPTION - HAITI - FOR PRIME MINISTER EVANS PAUL - PAUL ARMSTRONG

25/10/2016

Dear Deputy Head Of Mission - Mr. Rick Shearn,

This is my seventeenth email to you it concerns corruption in politics and the public experience of it. I want to work with you on bringing social justice to Haiti – especially I am concerned with the poor of Haiti. Please can you pass the following email onto Mr Evans Paul – Prime Minister of Haiti. I will be sending two more. If you have any ideas yourself [under the topic of the particular email] you can include them too. I enclose all my previous correspondence to you.

Thank You

Dear Prime Minister – Mr Evans Paul

I enclose my seventeenth email to you. It concerns corruption in politics and the public experience of corruption. The best idea out of this selection of ideas is an international court – financed by "United Nations Development Programme [UNDP] : Latin America and the Caribbean" for dealing with corruption in the country. Thank you for reading this email – I will write to you again – I also enclose all my previous correspondence to you.

CORRUPTION

- Invite bureaucrats to people's kitchens - less likely to be involved in corruption if they get to know the locals
- A branch within the police specifically to investigate corruption
- Get individual politicians across the political divide [different parties] to join together on combating corruption
- Business surveys to highlight levels of corruption

- Business can fill out government forms over the internet to avoid levels of corruption
- Politicians have to declare all their income sources [including you Mr. President]
- Media publicising corruption
- Rewards for reporting corruption if it shows to be true
- Judges are in charge of appointing senior civil service members
- A business integrity forum - to ensure businesses do not have to give bribes to people.
- Limit the amount of money businesses can give to political parties - all business may only donate to parties and not to individuals
- Politicians can register to have their finances investigated by the judiciary - Establish their credentials as "clean" politicians
- Politicians including the president cannot have shares or ownership over state assets<
- Establish a citizen report card - to survey citizens opinions / experiences of various state companies / state ministries. The results would be publicised in the media
- A UN workshop on corruption for politicians in a country
- A minister for corruption - drawn from civil society
- An international court in the country appointed by the AU to deal with corruption; validating elections - Reasons for this local judiciary is not skilled enough - concerns that local judiciary may not be as efficient due to lack of funding
- International police training for investigations / audits of people's finances
- Community groups - individuals joining together when seeking financing / applications for services - may reduce corruption
- NGO's can talk direct to the president about corruption
- Appointing judiciary with approval of parliament
- The public service proposes expenditure for government and then the government decides on it
- A tracking survey - how much of government funding budgeted for schools, health clinics etc. actually reaches them - citizens monitoring the budget
- Party financing must be made public - who supported them
- Political parties must have a party support base of people | must garner at least 1,000 signatures to form a party
- Political leaders must have their finances investigated
- Party base nominates those who can become politicians after any elections
- Protect those in the civil service who expose corruption
- Media presence at court cases | especially corruption cases
- Media can have access to public service to audit where money is being "lost" along the chain of bureaucracy
- Must vote for a party rather than individual politicians - reduces corruption such as buying votes / politicians doing favours for people
- Reform within the police by the police

- Making people aware of the consequences of corruption. They will be less likely to give in to corruption or accept it
- Force new legislation on corruption by gathering votes from across the political divide in parliament

#18 POLICE CORRUPTION - HAITI - FOR PRIME MINISTER EVANS PAUL - PAUL ARMSTRONG

25/11/2016

Dear Deputy Head Of Mission - Mr. Rick Shearn,

This is my eighteenth email to you it concerns corruption in the police and how to deal with it. I want to work with you on bringing social justice to Haiti – especially I am concerned with the poor of Haiti. Please can you pass the following email onto Mr Evans Paul – Prime Minister of Haiti. I will be sending one more. If you have any ideas yourself [under the topic of the particular email] you can include them too. I enclose all my previous correspondence to you.

Thank You

Dear Prime Minister – Mr Evans Paul

I enclose my eighteenth email to you. It concerns corruption in the police and ways of dealing with it. It places responsibility for proper policing in the hands of those most responsible. Thank you for taking the time to read this email – I will write to you again – I also enclose all my previous correspondence to you.

POLICE CORRUPTION

- Rotating police officers between districts to reduce corruption
- Vary police officers roles
- Full screening of backgrounds of recruits to the police force
- Candidates with higher levels of education should be sought and those who continue their education should be rewarded
- A use of a polygraph testing in initial screenings of candidates
- Police commanders are held personally responsible for their subordinates actions with regard to corruption
- Community policing begins after extensive training where police officers spend several days conducting surveys at each residence and business in their assigned neighborhood. There are two purposes for this 1. To introduce police officers to community residences and generate public interest 2. They provide officers with a preliminary assessment of the principal concerns specific to the community - providing info not just on citizen security but other social problems as well.
- An external commission to monitor police - independent of governance; must publicize findings

- Start from the top down. Police commanders must be seen visibly and persistently to lead reform
- Reinforce the message by personal visits to the rank and file police stations
- Reformers must think of ways to remind officers about what is expected in particular situations
- Signs can be placed at receiving counters at police stations that complaints must be registered without monetary charge
- Police should develop programs informing the public about anti-corruption initiatives and publicize procedures for complaining - This may raise anxiety among police officers that people will complain
- Police showing sincere efforts at reform will gain more respect from the public - giving them a sense of pride. Policing then becomes a vocation rather than a job
- Bring together police officer and civil society representatives to overcome a legacy of suspicion and fear. Participants in these dialogues exchange information about the sources of crime and violence and discussed ways that the police best re-establish control in the community. These dialogues should be renewed and continue

#19 FINANCING - HAITI - FOR PRIME MINISTER EVANS PAUL - PAUL ARMSTRONG

25/11/2016

Dear Deputy Head Of Mission - Mr. Rick Shearn,

This is my last email to you it concerns financing for the poor. I want to work with you on bringing social justice to Haiti – especially I am concerned with the poor of Haiti. Please can you pass the following email onto Mr Evans Paul – Prime Minister of Haiti. I will be sending one more. If you have any ideas yourself [under the topic of the particular email] you can include them too. I enclose all my previous correspondence to you.

Thank You

Dear Prime Minister – Mr Evans Paul

I enclose my last email to you dealing with social reform and justice. The ideas here are for improving the quality of life of the poor through various taxation methods and NGO financing methods. There may be some opposition to these ideas. Those who make up the small community of rich people in your country CAN afford these taxes – they are not severe. Be persistent on this – get this through legislation. Thank you for reading all my emails to you. I also enclose all my previous correspondence to you.

FINANCES

- A 5% tax for the poor on the middle and upper classes similar to the Muslim system of Zakat[5% also]

- A one-time wealth tax – for construction purposes
- Indigenous NGO's establishing offices in western countries for fundraising
- Get the president of Haiti involved - he should have a presidential fund which he can use to help others such as women and children
- Village leaders with more powers can raise a very small tax on local landlords

NUCLEAR WEAPONS

Purpose : To abolish all nuclear weapons in the world forever

Strategy : Pointing out that it is possible that nuclear weapons would be used

PAUL ARMSTRONG - TO REBECCA SHARKEY - NUCLEAR WEAPONS

5/04/2015

Dear Rebecca,

I sent the following email to the French embassy in Ireland for their president. Again – you can use these ideas without referencing me.

Paul Armstrong - Belorussia

Dear Ambassador

Please can you pass the following on to President Francois Hollande.

I am asking you to give up nuclear weapons. Belorussia is not highlighted in the media when it comes to a nuclear ban but it should. Here is an example of what would happen in a limited nuclear war. Genetic mutations in both humans, animals and plants would result – Mothers there are afraid to have children and the birth rate in that country has gone down[1]. The soil cannot be cleaned and many streams are unsafe – Children are taught songs about not going into the forests or drinking from streams[2]. It will take thousands of years before the country is any way safe again [3]. The brand name "produced in Belorussia" is a stigma – in agriculture it does not matter whether the food is safe or not no one would eat food from this country[4]. The real toll from Belorussia is far greater than admitted – cancers are not documented from those who were directly exposed to the radiation in the days after the explosion. A nuclear war would be the same – there is the immediate effect and then there is the legacy[5]. People have to continue with their lives – they cannot migrate en masse to another country – they have to live side by side with this effect – there is an oppressive attitude in the country – the same would be from a limited nuclear war [6].

PAUL ARMSTRONG - NUCLEAR ESCALATION

4/04/2015

Dear Ambassador,

Please can you pass the following on to your president.

If nuclear weapons are used there is a danger that friends of the targeted nation may respond with WMD themselves. It is either all or nothing - there will be more nuclear states or there will be no nuclear states. I'll tell you a secret - Isaiah prophesied a 1000 years of peace. That is not going to happen as we are now. Half the worlds out there do not make it and I am pretty sure that nuclear weapons were used in a lot of these cases. So if other worlds do it [destroy themselves] why not here. [1] War can escalate pretty fast. I do not believe nuclear weapons would be used immediately at the start of a war but they could if the war continued. Reasons for this would be too many casualties on your side [2]; a desire to end the war quickly and save soldiers by sacrificing millions of civilians in nuclear weapons strikes[3]. What I see is power interests; all nations are guilty of this to some degree and if there zone is challenged they will respond [4] - Again the issue of escalation. Nuclear weapons are going to be used eventually - Take that as a fact. The UK has stated that a threat to NATO would be a reason for strikes against others. [5] This is unthinkable considering the horrendous side-effects. Nuclear weapons do not prevent wars again an example of an escalation issue.[6]. There is an alternative an "escalation of disarmament". I do not see all nations agreeing all at once to disarm. It will happen in stages country by country. So I am working on you now along with Pakistan and India. Make this happen please. I will tell you who I will work on next after your country - China and the UK. Then Russia and then the rest. If one nation disarms another nation is more likely to do the same. If one nation holds on to weapons so will the other side[7]

PAUL ARMSTRONG - TO YOUR PRESIDENT

1/04/2015

So long as some nations have nuclear weapons others will want them. Some day it is going to destroy this planet - It will happen. There is only one way to save the world and that is all nations abolishing nuclear weapons forever. Some countries argue that having nuclear weapons is a sign of a mature and advanced society. What do you think? Are nuclear weapons evil - Could they cause catastrophic suffering even if used on a limmited scale. I fear this is how they will be used - tactical weapons. I rate it 60/40 at the moment that this will happen somewhere in the world within the next 40 years. For those affected by these weapons the suffering would be extreme. You have a responsibility for starting a cascade of nuclear disarmament in the world. Public opinion is against nuclear weapons and I hope this is the same in your country. I chose you - strategically to start this cascade. If you are an ambassador who opposes nuclear weapons please work with other politicians in your country to achieve this nuclear disarmament. Please also pass this email on to your president

RECOMMENDS

BOOKS / DOCUMENTS :

Book : "The Making Of An Islamic Political Leader - Conversations With Hasan Al-Turabi"
[Author : Mohamed E. Hamdi]

Book : Leading Diverse Communities : A How To Guide For Moving From Healing Into Action
[Authors : Cherie R. Brown | George J. Mazza | National Coalition Building Institute]

Document : Talking To Groups That Use Terror
[Editors : Nigel Quinney | A. Heather Coyne | USIP]

Document : Peace In Somaliland : An Indigenous Approach To State-Building
[Editors : Academy For Peace And Development [Somaliland]]

Document : Dangerous Liaisons With The Taliban : The Feasibility And Risks Of Negotiations
[Author : Matt Waldman | USIP]

Book : Getting It Right In Afghanistan
[Authors : Scott Smith; Moeed Yusuf; Colin Cookman [USIP]]

Book : Militias And The Challenge Of Post-Conflict Peace : Silencing The Guns
[Authors : Chris Alden; Monika Thakur; Matthew Arnold]

Toward Democratic Policing In Colombia : Institutional Accountability Through Lateral Reform
[Author : Eduardo Moncada [Comparative Politics]]

Document : Colombia's Peace Processes : Multiple Negotiations, Multiple Actors
[Authors : Cynthia J. Arnson; Jaime Bermudez; Father Dario Echeverri; David Henifin; Alfredo Rangel Suarez; Leon Valencia; | Woodrow Wilson International Centre For Scholars - Latin America Program]

Document : Participatory Budgeting : Core Principles And Key Impacts
[Author : Brian Wampler]

Book : Dictators And Dictatorships : Understanding Authoritarian Regimes And Their Leaders
[Authors : Natasha Ezrow; Erica Frantz]

Book : Deferring Democracy : Promoting Openness In Authoritarian Regimes
[Author : Catharin E. Dalpino]

Book : Partners For Democracy : Crafting The New Japanese State Under MacArthur
[Authors : Ray A. Moore; Donald L. Robinson]

Document : Media In Lebanon : Towards Enhancing Freedom Of Expression
[Author : Beyond Reform & Development]

Book : Syndromes Of Corruption : Wealth, Power, Democracy
[Author : Michael Johnston]

Book : Media In Transitional Democracies

[Author : Katrin Voltmer]

Document : Police Corruption : What Past Scandals Teach About Current Challenges

[Authors : David Bayley; Robert Perito; [USIP]]

Book : Creating Peace In Sri Lanka

[Editor : Rotberg]

Book : My Neighbor, My Enemy : Justice And Community In The Aftermath Of Mass Atrocity

[Editors : Eric Stover; Harvey M. Weinstein]

WEBSITES

Carl Medearis Website

http://www.carlmedearis.com

Conciliation Resources

http://www.c-r.org

Incore

http://www.incore.ulst.ac.uk/

International Peace Institute

http://www.ipacademy.org

United States Institute Of Peace

http://www.usip.org

Berghof Foundation

http://www.berghof-center.org/

International Alert

http://www.international-alert.org/

Beyond Reform And Development

http://www.beyondrd.com

www.ingramcontent.com/pod-product-compliance
Lightning Source LLC
Chambersburg PA
CBHW052032280526
45791CB00010B/2946